Kokushi-ryu
JUJUTSU

By Nobuyoshi Higashi

This is Kokushi-ryu Jujutsu

By Nobuyoshi Higashi, B.A., M.A. Head Instructor, Kokushi Budo Institute of New York, Inc. Associate Professor, State University of New York at Stony Brook. Founder (Soke), Kokushi-ryu Jujutsu. 7th Degree Black Belt Kodokan Judo, and 7th Degree Black Belt Aikido and Karate. Author of School Judo, Basic Judo, Advanced Judo, Kokushi-ryu Jujutsu, Karate-do, Aikido: Tradition and New Tomiki Free Fighting Method, Advanced Aikido, and Koryu Aikido. President, the United States Tomiki Aikido Association. President, International Kokushi-ryu Jujutsu Association.

Kokushi Budo Institute of New York, Inc.

ISBN: 0-86568-164-3
Library of Congress Catalog No.: 94-061146

UNIQUE PUBLICATIONS
4201 Vanowen Place
Burbank, California 91505

Contents

Preface

Jujutsu was first systematized at the end of the 16th century, and its development continued until the end of the 19th. In the late 1800's, the Tokugawa family was forced out of the shogunate, and Japan's feudal system collapsed. At that time, the Samurai (warriors) and the practice of jujutsu largely disappeared from Japanese culture, although a few people continued to study jujutsu.

Professor Jigoro Kano studied many jujutsu styles, and through the practice of old jujutsu, he discovered that it was good for both mental and physical fitness. In 1882, he selected some good jujutsu techniques, combined them with inventions derived from his own research, and established Kodokan judo as a sport. Since then, while judo has been developing throughout the world, jujutsu declined in popularity in Japan, although some jujutsu families have continued to practice jujutsu.

Today, however, jujutsu, too, is increasingly popular throughout the world. Few instructional materials and student guidelines are available, however. I studied the techniques and philosophy of old jujutsu and such current martial arts as judo, karate, kendo, and aikido. I then researched, organized, and established a jujutsu system based on modern educational principles.

I believe that jujutsu and academic education are of equal importance in the development of a student's mental health, moral character, and physical fitness. Through the practice of jujutsu, people learn the true value of the human spirit: love, respect, confidence, and joyful daily life. There are no racial tensions in their training; perhaps some day they can contribute their talents toward world peace.

In this book, the names of the basic techniques derive from current Kodokan judo, karate, and aikido so that students can learn the basic techniques of Kodokan judo, karate, and aikido as well.

My first priority is safety. In the teaching and practice of jujutsu our primary concern is to avoid accidents. Jujutsu is a physical contact activity which should be presented with a logical progression of techniques. Begin slowly and carefully with basic techniques and gradually progress to more complex techniques. You must know jujutsu safety rules, particularly to say, "I give up," as soon as you feel slight pain or discomfort when your opponent applies a joint-taking technique. Never wait to say, "I give up." If you don't want to fall down, tell your opponent not to throw you. Finally, you must study jujutsu with a qualified instructor.

I hope that both instructors and students will enjoy studying this book and will continue the practice of jujutsu as lifetime work.

I. What is Jujutsu?

Jujutsu is the Japanese art of attack and defense against an armed or unarmed opponent by grasping or striking so that the opponent's own strength and weight are used against him.

Modern jujutsu combines both physical and mental education. Through the practice of jujutsu, one learns skill, knowledge, and self-discipline while enjoying oneself. This develops a harmonious relationship between the physical and mental being, thus contributing to an individual's successful participation in society and his general education.

II. History of Jujutsu

Origin of Jujutsu

Before the advent of modern weapons, man needed a means of survival against his enemies. He taught himself to run, jump, throw, hold, punch, and kick. In this way, prehistoric man developed techniques that are employed in jujitsu, aikido, judo, karate, wrestling, and sumo.

Evidence in the authorized chronicle of Japan (Nihon Shoki) shows that a contest held in 230 B.C. was a close

1

contact martial arts fight. The contest was held between Takemi-kazuchi-no-kami and Takemi-nakata-no-kami. Takemi-kazuchi-no-kami took his opponent's arm joint and threw his opponent to the ground. He was made ruler as a reward. Another very bloody contest was hold between Nomino-sukune and Taimano-kehaya. Nomino-sukune hit his opponent's chest with his hand, threw his opponent onto the ground, and kicked him to death.

The account of these fights is the earliest record we have of jujutsu. Later, jujutsu (or yawara) appeared in literature in the "Once upon a time tales" (Konjaku-monogatari) of the 11th century. Over the centuries, jujutsu was called by such names as kumiuchi, kogusoku, taijutsu, wajutsu, torite, koshinomawari, hobaku, etc. Because the warriors of these accounts wore armor, the techniques consisted mainly of knocking down and then harming their opponents.

The contest of Nomino-sukune and Taimano-kehaya, from Ukiyo-e prints by Yoshitoshi (1839-1892).

In jujutsu, advanced techniques were developed from simple combat techniques. These advanced techniques were necessary for ancient warriors in the protection of their rulers' palaces. By utilizing jujutsu, the ancient warrior was able to protect himself in the event that he was unable to use a sword. The warrior studied and developed methods of punching, kicking, throwing, and taking joints.

The Golden Days of Jujutsu

Old jujutsu book (densho), author unknown, circa 1750.

Jujutsu became more formally organized in the latter half of the 16th century, and various ryu (schools or styles) were created between the 17th and 19th centuries. According to Tomiki,[1] There were 179th styles of jujutsu during this period. In those days, the warriors wore light dress, and many jujutsu techniques employed were joint techniques. Warriors trained for physical skill, but the building of one's character was of the utmost importance.

---

1. Kenji Tomiki, Goshinjutsu-nyumon (Tokyo: Seitosha, 1973), 27.

Descriptions of some jujutsu ryu, such as the Takenouchi-ryu, Kyushin-ryu, Kito-ryu, Tenshin-shinyo-ryu, and Daito-ryu, can show how they are related to present-day forms.

Takenouchi-ryu was founded by Takenouchi Nakatsukasadayu Hisamori (1469-1561) in 1532. This school specialized in rope and holding techniques. Twenty-one vital spots (kyusho) were illustrated by this school.

Kyushin-ryu was founded by Inugami Sakon Shogen Nagakatsu during the Eiroku era (1558-1569). He wrote a book explaining basic principles, including Atemi (attacks on the vital spots by hand or foot) and Kappo (methods of resuscitation).

Sekiguchi-ryu was founded by Sekiguchi Yarokusaemon Ujishin (1597-1670) in the Tokugawa Iemitsu era (1624-1643). This school used two teaching methods: one was a general practice without weapons, and the other included actual fighting methods, with students wearing armor and using weapons.

Kito-ryu was founded by Ibaragi Sensai Toshifusa (1597-1670) in the Tokugawa-Iemitsu era (1624-1643). This school established the order of training methods. For example, Omote-no-kata (the forms of part and counterpart) has seven techniques. Students practiced the techniques, from the elementary to the more advanced, following the order of the school. This school had outstanding throwing techniques and emphasized mental training. Judo throwing techniques are based on this school's methods. The present Kodokan's (Judo headquarters) Koshiki-no-kata (the "antique form") were originated by the Kito-ryu, and this kata (form) has 21 techniques.

Tenshin-shinyo-ryu was founded by Iso Mataemon Masaashi at the end of the Tokugawa era (1861-1864). This school was one of the biggest schools at the end of the feudal era and has excellent katame-waza (the art of holding, choking, and joint techniques) and atemi-waza (the art of punching and kicking techniques). Judo's katame-waza and atemi-waza are based on these methods.

Daito-ryu was founded by Minamoto Shinra Saburo Yoshimitsu (died 1127). After some time, this style was adapted by the Takeda family of the Aizu clan. During the Meiji period (1868-1911), it was introduced by Takeda Sokaku to the general population. This school had the best joint techniques as well as atemi-waza (punching and kicking). Aikido techniques are based on this school's methods.

Documents show that jujutsu techniques had been developed by the successive generations of the founding families. However, since instruction was kept secret, techniques within each school remained very limited. For example, one school specialized in throwing techniques while another emphasized joint techniques.

The Meiji period (1868-1911)

In 1868, the feudal system collapsed in Japan, and imperial rule was restored. Old cultural and social systems disappeared and were replaced by new systems and cultures from foreign countries. Warriors (samurai) were no longer in existence, and the wearing of swords was prohibited. Jujutsu and other martial arts had been studied mainly by the samurai, and with those samurai the martial arts were disappearing as well. However, a small number of schools were maintained by certain families.

Professor Jigoro Kano (1860-1938), the originator of judo, realized that jujutsu was good for both mind and body, and consequently studied and researched several different styles of jujutsu. He then founded Kodokan Judo in 1882.

In 1883, with society changing, jujutsu masters were employed by the Tokyo police department to teach policemen. For several years thereafter there was a renaissance in the art.

Between 1885 and 1887, contests were conducted by the Tokyo police department, and the newly formed Kodokan Judo made a strong showing by winning many contests against jujutsu players. Jujutsu again disappeared from the Japanese scene until more recent times. Because jujutsu players lost against judo players from the newly formed Kodokan, judo became recognized by Japanese society, and Kodokan judo became the principal martial art in Japan. The spread of judo has led to its admission in the Olympic games since 1964.

Why did jujutsu players lose the contests? They stayed strictly within the limits of the old system while the practice of judo became more scientific and included free practice (randori). In addition, no hitting or kicking was allowed while judo and jujutsu players were having contests. Had the rules permitted the hitting and kicking techniques, the results might have been quite different.

Modern Jujutsu

With the increasing crime rate in a sedentary society, people began to seek a means of self-defense that would give them adequate exercise. Once again, jujutsu appeared as a means of self-defense.

III. Kokushi-ryu Jujutsu

Education is the most important factor in our lives because the future of scientific development and the knowledge of human needs depends on it. Modern jujutsu is an education in and of itself. Through practice, jujutsu helps develop good citizenship, responsibility, and leadership. It fosters honesty, courage, and creativity, along with a positive attitude, strong moral character, and physical fitness. Jujutsu practice helps one to protect oneself from natural and manmade hazards, from sickness, and from human attack.

Urban crime has been growing at a rapid rate. At the same time, many people have developed low self-esteem. These people need to protect themselves and to build self-confidence and physical fitness. I wanted to meet their need for the development of the mind, personality, honesty, courage, and the skills of self-defense with enjoyable exercise.

I studied many different martial arts, including ancient jujutsu, judo, karate, aikido, kendo, and others. After investigating and scientifically researching the martial arts for many years, I strongly realized the need for jujutsu as a system of education and self-defense. Then, I reorganized the ancient techniques and joined them with the modern martial arts. In January, 1965, I established Kokushi-ryu Jujutsu, which incorporates all these ideas with the best educational theory. Through the practice of jujutsu, students find enjoyment in mental and physical fitness as well as increased confidence in dealing with everyday life.

Jujutsu techniques were formed centuries ago, but some techniques remain basically unchanged today. The ancient jujutsu had only formal practice and discipline without enjoyment. For example, only one side was permitted to attack at a time. But the modern jujutsu that I have developed has both formal and free practice. For example, free practice means both sides can attack simultaneously; also, modern jujutsu techniques give protection against modern weapons such as guns. Most importantly, everybody can develop skill and self-discipline with enjoyment.

The meaning of Kokushi-ryu Jujutsu is as follows: Kokushi is a loyal warrior, ryu is a style, jujutsu is human education. It is the first modernized and organized jujutsu and educational system in the world. Each student can learn freely at his own pace and enjoy practice while learning self-discipline. This style of jujutsu includes throwing, punching, kicking, joint-taking, and mind development; all of these are equally important in the practice of jujutsu.

Physiologists often set age limits for many sports activities, but there are no age limits in jujutsu. Thus, everyone can continue for as long as they enjoy it. For example, there are people over 70 years old practicing jujutsu, and they do so at a high level of physical performance.

Jujutsu fulfills a broad range of needs for individuals in our society; because of its diverse benefits and its contribution to physical and mental health, it will inevitably become the best martial art in the world.

Our school has a dojo-kun (slogan or oath). Since it is very hard to translate directly, we use the Japanese words: (1) seii, (2) kinro, (3) kenshiki, and (4) kihaku. These words can be defined as follows:

(1) Seii

The most important concepts contained in the word Seii are sincerity, faith, and trust. To make a sincere friendship and to place one's trust in another person is Seii manifested. But the ideas of confidence, honesty, hope, and love are also part of Seii.

11

(2) Kinro

Kinro is labor, endeavor, and exertion. It is a lavished labor, a labor that is necessary and useful. Kinro is an active and altruistic endeavor. It is an energetic effort made to attain a goal. Kinro is exertion and requires one to continue unremittingly, exploiting one's total mental and physical abilities.

(3) Kenshiki

Knowledge, insight, dignity, and awareness form the basis of Kenshiki. Knowledge is not only accumulated, it deepens as one attempts to understand modern society and as new knowledge is discovered. Its use is a necessity for one's future triumphs. Kenshiki is not knowledge alone. It is embodied in the person of insight, the person who has a keen, remarkable insight into human nature. Kenshiki combines knowledge and insight with dignity - a calm dignity, the dignity of human worth.

(4) Kihaku

Spirit is the most meaningful translation of Kihaku. One must learn to cultivate the spirit of fair play, loyalty, friendship, and honorable peace. Kihaku is the display of spirit, poise, and courage in the face of danger. It is the nurturing of human independence, responsibility, and inquiry. Kihaku fosters courage and the cultivation of vitality.

IV. The Values of Jujutsu

There are five major values of jujutsu practice: 1. Physical development, 2. Mental development, 3. Social development, 4. Self-defense, and 5. Lifetime sport.

1. Physical Development

Through the various movements of jujutsu techniques, such as throwing, being thrown, grappling, twisting joints, punching, kicking, choking, escaping, falling, and bending, the body builds up its physical strength and fitness. These activities also develop the systems of the internal organs, such as the circulatory, excretory, respiratory, cardiac regulation, and digestive systems, etc. Today's lifestyles require people to be physically fit if they are to perform efficiently. Through practicing jujutsu, they can identify individual fitness needs, develop self-confidence, and become mentally and physically healthy people who enjoy life without illness. Nerves and muscles are inseparable. Without nerves, muscles are incapable of voluntary movement. The central nervous system controls the entire body and makes one capable of movement, be it moving the head, arms, legs, or other parts of the body in walking, running, etc. Jujutsu practice requires the perfect movement of the body in situations of escaping, defending, and attacking. For example, if a person apples a front kick (mae-geri) at you, you may be knocked out by his kick, or your arm may be damaged by blocking if you stay in one spot and do not move. But, if you execute a proper escape to avoid the kick, you need minimum power to counter the attack effectively. We train for and practice mainly this type of movement. As a result, you develop the coordination of nerves and muscles.

2. Mental Development

There are a great many methods of attack and defense in jujutsu. The student must have knowledge of the rules, good judgment, accuracy in body movement, understanding of the strategy of attack and defense, and the ability to redirect the power of an opponent.

Jujutsu is a fighting art. If one is ignorant of the rules of practice, one may kill an opponent, break his joints, or inflict damage to other parts of his body. In practice, for example, should an opponent try to apply a choke, one must escape and counterattack by striking at the opponent's face, arresting one's fist several inches from his face in order to avoid injury.

Good judgment controls the student's activity. For example, he must gauge the optimal distance from his attacker, namely, the distance best suited for counterattack or escape. He will avoid being approached from behind and fighting with the sun in his eyes. When walking along the street, he knows instinctively how to prepare his mind and body for defense against approaching danger.

In addition to a knowledge of the rules and techniques of jujutsu, the student learns responsibility toward other students and develops good judgment in the course of practicing this art. He learns to attack and defend effectively, to interpret an assault, and to counterattack with a calm and fearless spirit. Such development of mind and spirit enables the student to make rapid decisions in highly emotional situations, such as being attacked on the street, or in other times of stress or crisis.

3. Social Development

A class is usually composed of racially, socially, and physically varied people. Each individual has different opinions, strengths, and life experiences. The person who enrolls in a class needs to adjust to the other students as individuals and as a group. Through jujutsu practice, the student in this society-within-a-society develops human relationships, leans new rules, and becomes a socially fit individual. Jujutsu practice offers one of the best opportunities to train in human relations. For example, if one breaks the rules of practice, the result can be an injury to oneself or one's partner. But these students are constantly guided and helped by other students so that the rules of the practices are gradually learned and friendship is fostered. As

16

a rule, advanced students must teach or help beginners. All students are expected to attend class regularly and punctually, thereby learning responsibility toward one another, self-confidence, and leadership abilities.

The physical contact of jujutsu necessitates cooperation. Since the students are constantly engaged in cooperative practice with one another, they develop a feeling of belonging and being a part of the whole. Honesty, courtesy, sympathy, partnership, and fairness come naturally and lead to self-respect and respect for others. Jujutsu practice is itself the jujutsu society. The jujutsu society is the society-within-a-society that contributes to the happiness in the player's daily life, which in turn contributes to the welfare of the greater society. It is through the practice of jujutsu that we can reach out to each other and build a more peaceful, loving coexistence in the world.

4. Self-defense

Jujutsu is a method of attack and defense that is very valuable for self-defense. These days we need to protect ourselves from muggers or other attackers.

Through the practice of jujutsu, you learn the basic defense methods:

(1) Discover and avoid a threat before your opponent attacks you. For example, if you are walking down the street, and a stranger is approaching whom you feel may

attack you; if someone is hiding on the corner; or if any situation occurs where you feel the possibility of danger, avoid the threat by changing directions instead of going through that area so that you may avoid the attacker (I call this having a feeling for discovery). Avoiding such situations is the most important self-defense.

(2) You must attack before your opponent attacks you. For example, if your opponent's eyes are somewhat glassy, he may be a drug user, or he may be so angry that you feel he may kill you; in either case, do not wait - you must attack before your opponent attacks you (I call this having a feeling for defense).

(3) Defend against various attacks with or without a weapon. Sometimes, it is impossible to avoid a situation of human attack. If your attacker wants only money, you can give him money so that he will not harm you; this is the best defense. However, if he tries to harm or kill you, are you going to give up your life? No, you must defend yourself. In this situation, jujutsu has over a thousand defense methods or techniques that you can apply.

Through the practice of jujutsu, you will gain confidence and enjoy everyday life without fear of anybody. Confidence helps you to avoid situations where a mugger is going to attack you and helps you to deal successfully with situations where an attack cannot be anticipated and avoided.

5. Lifetime Sport

Jujutsu techniques are interesting enough to be enjoyed during your leisure throughout a lifetime. These activities contribute to the individual's physical, mental, and social welfare, and serve as an outlet for competitiveness.

Physical skills are not developed in several lessons; it takes months and even years of repeated practice to become skillful in even the simplest foot movements. Students, of course, vary in body structure, power, and knowledge. Some people progress faster than others, so that the students provide their own individual goals and accomplishments. As the students begin to see the development of their skills, they begin to enjoy participating in jujutsu.

Jujutsu has a ranking system similar to other martial arts. For example, the beginner is designated by wearing a white belt. After practicing several months, certain skills are developed, and the student is promoted to the next rank of yellow belt, etc. This ranking system gives students concrete recognition of their increased skills and permits them to take greater pride in their achievement.

V. Knowledge of jujutsu

When one practices jujutsu, one should understand: A. The bow (rei), B. Methods of practice (renshu-ho), C. Exercise hall (dojo), D. Hygiene (ei-sei), E. Jujutsu uniform (jujutsu-gi), and F. Vital spots of the human body (kyusho). In this way, good manners and appropriate attitude are developed in class along with the internal knowledge of jujutsu.

A. The bow (rei)

The bow is an expression of respect for the opponent. The bow is performed when entering or leaving the exercise hall and when meeting people. We also bow to the instructor and to each other before and after practice. There are two forms of bowing in jujutsu. One is the standing bow, and the other is the kneeling bow.

Standing bow (tachi-rei)

Assume a natural stance, and face each other.

Bend your upper body forward until a forty-five degree angle is reached. Then, return to your original position. The duration of the bow is about two seconds from start to finish.

Kneeling bow (za-rei)

The kneeling bow should be practiced in combination with the art of sitting and the art of standing up.

Art of sitting (suwari-kata): From the basic natural stance, kneel on your left knee by placing the left knee on the spot vacated by ball of the left foot. The knee and ball of your left foot should be in contact with the mat.

Next, lower your right knee to the spot vacated by the ball of your right foot. The knee and ball of your right foot should be in contact with the mat. The knees should be about thirty-five degrees apart. Then, extend your toes, and place the big toes on top of each other. Your feet are now resting on the insteps. Lower your hips onto your calves and feet. Hold your torso erect, and place your hands on the middle of your upper thighs. The fingers are closed, pointing diagonally inward (sitting position or sei-za).

The kneeling bow (za-rei): Place both hands on the mat, about two fists apart, in front of your knees. Bend your upper body forward about thirty-five degrees, and return to a sitting position. The duration of the bow is about two seconds from start to finish.

The art of standing up (tachi-kata): From a sitting position, elevate your hips, and shift your weight to your knees. Bend the ankles so that the ball of your feet make contact with the mat. Next, lift your right knee, and place the boll of your right foot on the vacated spot. Do the same with your left knee, and stand in basic natural stance.

B. Methods of practice (renshu-ho)

1. Exercise for warming up (junbi-undo)

The human body needs to warm up. Stretch your muscles, and bend and twist your body. This relaxes the entire body in preparation for any kind of strenuous technique. Exercises should be related to the jujutsu techniques.

2. Practice basic movements (kihon-dosa) and basic techniques (kihon-waza)

First, you should practice basic movements and basic techniques so that you can incorporate these movements and techniques into your overall practice of jujutsu.

3. Form practice (kihon-no-kata)

All of the movements of the practice are arranged in a pattern of attack and defense. Your opponent attacks slowly, and you apply techniques slowly and correctly so that both participants can understand the techniques. Repeat slowly until you understand the techniques. Next, both you and your opponent practice with speed.

4. Free practice (jiyu-renshu)

When you have mastered the individual techniques by studying the forms, your opponent attacks from any direction without warning, and you then apply a technique.

5. Serious fight (shinken-shobu)

When you become involved in a serious fight, you may become emotional and afraid. In order to calm down, you must use the mental power, skill, judgment, and physical strength that you have learned. Do not wait for your opponent's attack. You must take the initiative. For example, when you see your opponent's fist or an attacking motion, you should attack faster than your opponent.

Our style of jujutsu features the contest (shiai), which I have substituted for a serious fighting situation.

C. Exercise hall (dojo)

The exercise hall is the place for physical and mental training. You should bow both before entering and before leaving the hall. When in the exercise hall, show good manners by quietly standing at the side of the hall. Always keep your eyes on the players who are practicing jujutsu, so that you may learn new techniques from them. Before leaving, you should always clean the hall.

D. Hygiene (ei-sei)

Jujutsu is a physical contact martial art. Therefore, you must keep your uniform clean, cut your nails, and keep your exercise hall clean. Workouts are very strenuous, so you should not eat for one hour before practice.

E. Jujutsu uniform (jujutsu-gi)

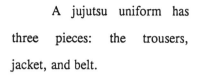

A jujutsu uniform has three pieces: the trousers, jacket, and belt.

How to wear the uniform: Put on the trousers and adjust the belt-cord. Put the belt-cord through the loops and tie it in front. Next, put the jacket on; the left flap covers the right. Place the center of the belt in front of your abdomen, and wrap it around your waist. Tie both ends in front of your abdomen with a double knot.

F. Vital spots of the human body (kyusho)

If you hit or kick certain areas of your opponent's body, the opponent may die, be rendered unconscious, or become partially paralyzed. The target area for such a blow is called a vital spot (kyusho).

There are 65 vital spots in the human body.[1] Those named here are the most effective and are used in jujutsu.

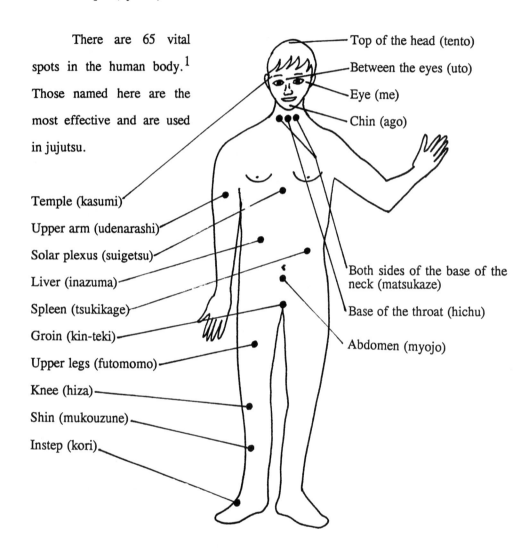

Top of the head (tento)

Between the eyes (uto)

Eye (me)

Chin (ago)

Temple (kasumi)

Upper arm (udenarashi)

Solar plexus (suigetsu)

Liver (inazuma)

Spleen (tsukikage)

Groin (kin-teki)

Upper legs (futomomo)

Knee (hiza)

Shin (mukouzune)

Instep (kori)

Both sides of the base of the neck (matsukaze)

Base of the throat (hichu)

Abdomen (myojo)

---

1. Takaaki Asami, and Yoshizo Matsumoto, "Studies on the Vital Spots of the Human body," Bulletin of the Association for the Scientific Studies on Judo (Tokyo: Kodokan, Report IV, 1972), 61-81.

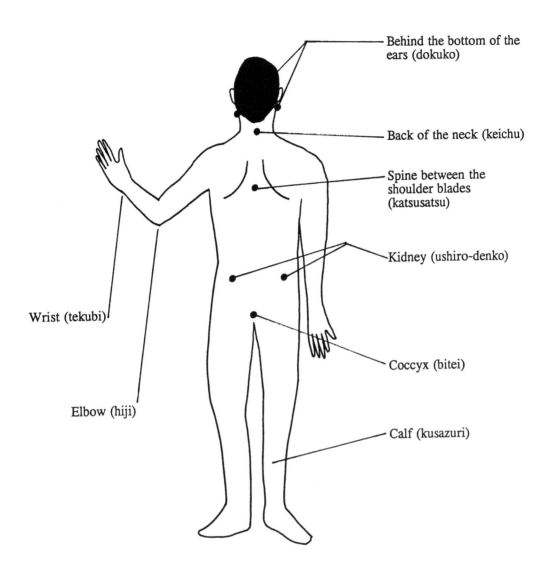

Behind the bottom of the ears (dokuko)

Back of the neck (keichu)

Spine between the shoulder blades (katsusatsu)

Kidney (ushiro-denko)

Wrist (tekubi)

Coccyx (bitei)

Elbow (hiji)

Calf (kusazuri)

VI. Basic Movements (kihon-dosa)

A. Stance (tachi-kata)

When assuming a stance, it is vital that your body maintain flexibility. This enables you to act spontaneously and with ease in either an attack or a defense situation.

Natural stance (shizen-dachi)

Natural stance is standing naturally with feet shoulder-width apart and weight on both feet.

Right natural stance (migi-shizen-dachi)

Right natural stance is standing naturally with right foot forward and weight on both feet.

Left natural stance (hidari-shizen-dachi)

Left natural stance is standing naturally with left foot forward and weight on both feet.

Back stance (kokutsu-dachi)

From natural stance, advance the left foot one pace forward and bend both knees and raise the left heel from floor. Distribute your weight, putting 70% on the rear leg and 30% on the front leg. Now, pull backward and twist your hips slightly toward the right (left back stance). For right back stance, just reverse your position.

Forward stance (zenkutsu-dachi)

From natural stance, advance the left foot two paces forward and bend the left knee. Keep the back leg straight and your upper body erect (left forward stance). For right forward stance, just reverse the position.

Horse stance (kiba-dachi)

From natural stance, move the right foot one step to the right. Bend your knees and spread them outward until the knees are over your big toes. Keep your upper body straight.

Toes inward stance (haji-dachi)

From natural stance, rotate your heels outward so that your toes point inward at a 45 degree angle. Push your knees outward, tightening the muscles of the upper thighs, buttocks, and abdomen. Your shoulders should be relaxed.

Fighting stance (shobu-dachi)

From natural stance, advance the left foot one pace forward and bend both knees slightly. The toes of your left foot point straight forward. The right foot is turned facing 45 degrees to the right. At this time, your body weight is distributed equally on both feet (left fighting stance). The upper body should be turned slightly to the right. For right fighting stance, just reverse the position.

B. Distance (maai)

You should always be able to keep an idea in your mind of the proper distance to be maintained between you and your opponent during attack and defense. The proper distance is the distance that allows you to attack easily that prevents your opponent from attacking easily. Stepping forward with your right or left foot closes the distance between the two of you. Now, you are in position to apply the techniques on your opponent. This is the best distance for far-distance fighting.

C. Eye contact (metsuke)

Watch your opponent's face calmly so that your peripheral vision enables you to see your opponent from head to foot. Do not stare at your opponent. If you stare at his right hand, you may not see your opponent's left hand or his feet. Thus, he can attack you with the left hand or with his feet. If you train hard, some day you will be able to read your opponent's thoughts with your mind's eye.

D. Breath control (kokyu-ho)

Do not inhale while attacking or blocking a blow that is being delivered by your opponent. Recent research has indicated that if you scream, "Exhale!" as you punch the target, your power will be increased. So, you should exhale while you attack or defend.

E. The body as a weapon (karada-no-buki)

The body itself provides weapons that can be used as the situation demands. The weapons in jujutsu are parts of the body, such as the hands, arms, leg, shoulders, head, and trunk.

Here, I have selected for illustration those body parts most commonly used as weapons. These are: 1. Hands, 2. Arms, 3. Legs, and 4. Head.

1. Hands (te)

Fist (ken)

To make a fist, fold all your fingers as tightly as you can at the second joint. Next, continue bending the fingers until they press into the palms. Then, bend your thumb down on top of them, snugly.

Striking is done with the knuckles of the index and middle fingers. This is called the forefist or seiken. The fist is your most important weapon and can be used on any part of your opponent's body, such as the face, stomach, and kidneys.

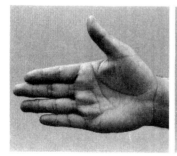   

Knife-hand (shuto)

The knife-hand is made by stretching your fingers out, holding them together tightly, and bending the thumb slightly inward. Next, bend the hand slightly toward your thumb. The striking part of the hand is the outer edge of the wrist bone and the medial surface of the heel of the hand.

The knife-hand is used to strike at the face, head, neck, shoulder, kidney, and groin, additionally for blocking punches and kicks.

Palm-heel (shotei)

Open your hand, and bend the hand backward. The striking portion of the hand is the base of your palm. This shotei (palm-heel) is useful in attacks to the chin and groin and for blocking punches and kicks.

Spear-hand (nukite)

Open the hand, but keep the finger joints slightly bent extending your power to the fingertips. The striking portion of the hand is the fingertips. This spear-hand is useful for attacking your opponent's eyes and body.

35

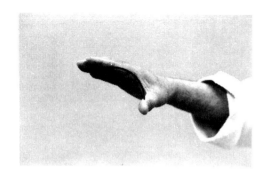

Crescent-hand (mikazukite)

Keep the four fingers of the hand close together with the thumb widely opposed to them and the palm facing down. The striking part is the curved area between the index finger and the thumb. This crescent-hand is useful in attacks to the neck.

2. Arms (ude)

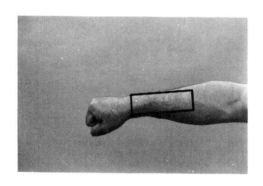

Forearm (kote)

The striking area is the forearm. This part of the body is useful in attacks to your opponent's temple and neck, after which a throwing technique may be used.

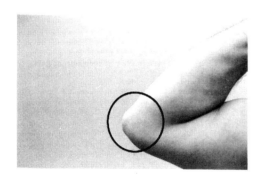

Elbow (hiji)

By bending your arm tightly, you will be able to use any part of the elbow in any direction: upward, downward, and sideways. The elbow is used to attack your opponent's face and other parts of the body. This is useful in close-distance fighting.

3. Leg (ashi)

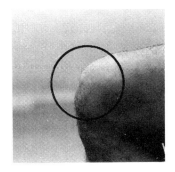

Knee (hiza)

The knee is used to strike the groin, stomach, and face. This is good in close-contact fighting.

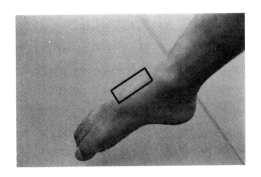

Instep (haisoku)

The instep is the top surface of the foot, opposite your arch. This is useful for striking the groin and the face.

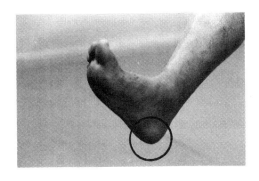

Heel (kakato)

The heel is used for the back kick. It is also used in stomping your opponent when he is lying on the ground.

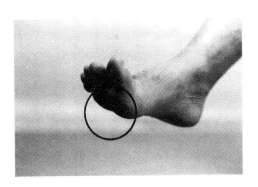

Ball of the foot (chusoku)

The ball of the foot is used with the front kick and round kick. When using the ball of the foot, keep the toes stretched upward as far as possible. The ball of the foot is used when attacking the stomach, chin, face, and ribs.

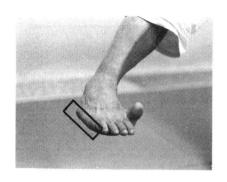

Knife-foot (sokuto)

The striking area is the outer edge of the foot. The knife-foot is used for the side kick to the knee, stomach, neck, and face.

4. Head (atama)

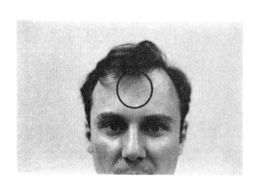

The portions of the head used in striking are the front (the forehead), the side (above the ears), and the back (well above the neck). The head strikes against your opponent's face.

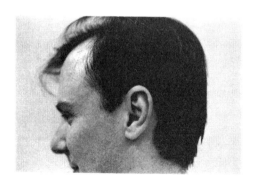

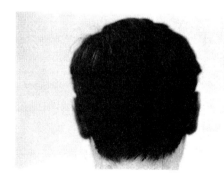

F. Foot movements (unsoku)

Foot movements are among the most important basic jujutsu techniques. You move your body straight forward, backward, sideways and diagonally. They are especially valuable as a defense against frontal attacks involving punches, kicks, and weapons. Accuracy of foot movements can enable you to escape from an attack without having been touched and without having to use power. Good foot movement enables you to attack or defend more effectively as well.

Key points

1. You must look at his entire body when you move your feet.

2. Your feet should slide as close to the ground as possible.

3. Maintain your center of gravity in the same place.

4. Your body weight should be on the foot that moves.

5. Move with mind, body, and feet in total coordination.

6. Read your opponent's distance.

7. Find out whether your opponent has weapons or is barehanded.

Practice 1 from natural stance

There are fourteen different ways of moving:

1) Move one step to the front with your left foot, then right foot into left natural stance. Next, move one step to the rear with your right foot, then left foot into natural stance (original stance).

2) Move one step diagonally to the left front with your left foot, then right foot into left natural stance. Simultaneously, turn your body slightly to the right. Next, move one step diagonally to the right rear with your right foot, then left foot into natural stance.

3) Move one step diagonally to the left front with your right foot, then left foot into right natural stance. Simultaneously, turn your body slightly to the right. Next, move one step diagonally to the right rear with your left foot, then right foot into natural stance.

4) Move one step to the left with your left foot, then right foot into natural stance. Simultaneously, turn your body slightly to the right. Next, move one step to the right with your right foot, then left foot into natural stance.

5) Move one step diagonally to the left rear with your left foot, then right foot into right natural stance. Simultaneously, turn your body slightly to the right. Next, move one step diagonally to the right front with your right foot, then left foot into natural stance.

6) Move one step diagonally to the left rear with your right foot, then left foot into left natural stance. Simultaneously, turn your body slightly to the right. Next, move one step diagonally to the right front with your left foot, then right foot into natural stance.

7) Move one step to the rear with your left foot, then right foot into right natural stance. Next, move one step to the front with your right foot, then left foot into natural stance.

Repeat on the opposite side.

Practice 2 from natural stance

Practice foot movement simultaneously with the hand blocking methods, that is, the upper, middle, and lower blocks. Recommended routine practice (utilizing foot movement from practice 1):

1) Left lower block (hidari gedan-uke).

2) Left middle outside block (hidari chudan-soto-uke).

3) Right middle inside block (migi chudan-uchi-uke).

4) Right lower block (migi gedan-uke).

5) Right lower block (migi gedan-uke).

6) Left upper outside block (hidari jodan-soto-uke).

7) Right upper block (migi jodan-uke).

     Repeat on the opposite side.

43

Practice 3 from natural stance

Practice foot movement while simultaneously blocking and punching. Recommended routine practice (utilizing foot movement from practice 1):

1) Left lower block and right middle thrust (migi chudan-tsuki).

2) Left middle outside block and right upper thrust (migi jodan-tsuki).

3) Right middle inside block and right crescent-hand thrust (migi mikazukite-tsuki).

4) Right lower block and left upper thrust (hidari jodan-tsuki).

5) Right lower block and right fist upper strike (migi ken-jodan-uchi).

6) Left upper outside block and left knife-hand horizontal strike (shuto-suihei-uchi).

7) Right upper block and left upper thrust (hidari jodan-tsuki).

Repeat on the opposite side.

Practice 4 from left (or right) fighting stance

Practice foot movement while simultaneously blocking and kicking. Recommended routine practice (utilizing foot movement from practice 1):

1) Left lower block and right front kick (migi mae-geri).

2) Left middle outside block and right round kick (migi mawashi-geri).

3) Right middle inside block and left back spin kick (hidari ushiro-mawashi-geri).

4) Right lower block and right side kick (migi yoko-geri).

5) Right lower block and right side kick (migi yoko-geri).

6) Left upper outside block and left back kick (hidari ushiro-geri)

7) Right upper block and right front kick (migi mae-geri).

Repeat on the opposite side.

G. Breakfall (ukemi)

Breakfall is the art of falling down safely without shock or injury when you fall by yourself or when thrown by your opponent. It is extremely important to learn to breakfall before studying any throwing techniques. By studying diligently, the student will gain confidence in falling and thereby learn jujutsu techniques much faster.

Breakfall has four basic directions: 1. Falling backward (ushiro-no-ukemi), 2. Falling sideways (yoko-no-ukemi), 3. Falling straight forward (mamae-no-ukemi), and 4. Falling forward with roll-out (zenpo-kaiten-ukemi).

1. Falling backward (ushiro-no-ukemi)

When falling backward, one must protect the back of the head and the back of the body.

Practice I

From a supine position, raise your arms to shoulder height and raise your head. Next, hit the mat with both arms simultaneously (using the entire length of the arm and the palms). Each arm makes a forty degree angle from your body, and your fingers are together (open hand).

Practice II

From a standing position, using a natural stance, raise the arms to shoulder height. Next, bend your knees, bringing your hips close to your heels. Roll backward, and keep your chin tucked close to your chest so that your head does not strike the mat. Before your back touches the mat, hit the mat with both arms at a forty degree angle from your body (using arms and palms). Your fingers are together (open hand). When your back touches the mat, both legs are raised and extended upward.

2. Falling sideways (yoko-no-ukemi)

When falling sideways, one must protect the shoulder and arm.

Practice I

Lie on the mat in a left side position. Your left side, including the lateral side of the left leg and foot, is in contact with the mat. Your legs are shoulder-width apart, with knees slightly bent. The right foot is in full contact with the mat, and the right knee is pointing diagonally towards your left side. Do not cross your legs. Your left arm is resting on the mat at a forty degree angle from your body. Raise your right arm level with your right shoulder. Next, raise your legs and turn your entire body to the right. At the same time, hit the mat with your right arm at a forty degree angle from your body (using the length of the arm and the palm), and drop your legs. Now, your body and limbs should be in the exact opposite position of that in which you began.

Repeat this exercise from a right side position.

Practice II

From a standing position using a natural stance, raise your right arm forward to shoulder height. Next, extend your right foot forward and to the left (moving it in front of your left foot), and bend your left knee until your hips are close to your left heel. Then, fall to your right, and hit the mat with your right arm at a forty degree angle from your body.

Repeat this exercise on the opposite side.

3. Falling straight forward (mamae-no-ukemi)

When falling straight forward, one must protect the face, chest, stomach, and knees.

Practice I

From a kneeling position with hips elevated above your heels and body straight, bend your elbows, keeping the palms turned away from your face. Keep a distance of twelve inches between your face and hands. Hold your hands slightly cupped, with the fingers making a forty-five degree angle. The elbows are held away from the body. Then, fall forward, and hit the mat with your forearms and palms. In your final position you will be supporting yourself on your knees and forearms and palms, with the rest of your body elevated above the mat.

Practice II

From standing position using a natural stance, fall forward, keeping your body straight. Use the same procedure as in practice I. In your final position you will be supporting your body on your toes, forearms, and palms, with the rest of your body elevated above the mat.

4. Falling forward with roll-out (zenpo-kaiten-ukemi)

When doing a falling forward with roll-out, one must protect the head, neck, and shoulders.

Practice I

From a standing position using a natural stance, place your right foot one step forward, and bend both knees, bringing you to a squatting position. Next, place your left hand on the mat in front of your left foot and parallel to your right foot, with the fingers pointing to the right. Then, place your right hand on the mat between your left hand and your right foot, with the fingers pointing inward. Turn your head to the left, and roll forward by pushing your body forward with pressure from your left foot against the mat. At the start of the roll, contact with the mat should be in the following order: outer surface of right arm, right shoulder, back, left hip, left leg, and right foot. At the completion of the roll, hit the mat with your left arm and palm. In the final position, your legs should be extended and parallel to one another, with knees slightly bent. Do not cross your legs.

Practice on the opposite side.

Practice II

From a standing position using a natural stance, place your right foot one step forward, and bend forward. Then, follow through as in practice I.

H. Resuscitation method (kappo)

Kappo is a method of resuscitation from unconsciousness caused by a choking technique during practice or a real fight.

Kappo was started by the Musso school of jujutsu during the 16th century.* Present-day kappo has been scientifically researched and has proven to be of great effectiveness.

Martial art instructors and black belt holders should know the kappo, so that when a student is unconscious from a choking technique, the kappo can be applied as fast as possible. To do so, you apply pressure to the student's chest or abdomen so that the student resumes normal respiration.

When the student is unconscious from a punch or kick, you should not touch or lift him. Call the doctor immediately, because there may be serious injury to his internal organs.

There are two kinds of kappo: one is respiratory kappo (kokyu-katsu), and the other is testicle kappo (kogan-katsu).

1. Respiratory kappo (kokyu-katsu)

This is used to wake up the student who is unconscious because of choking techniques. The most practical and useful techniques are the inductive method (sasoi-katsu), the aggregate method (so-katsu), and the back abdomen method (ura-katsu).

Inductive method (sasoi-katsu)

Place the victim in a sitting position, with his legs stretched apart. Next, support the victim's upper body from behind with your right kneecap. Place both your open hands (palm down) on his chest, and press his chest downward and then release it, so that air is

*Ikai, M, M. Tezuka, T. Sasa, Y. Matsumoto, T. Asami, T. Kawamura, and M. Kaneko, "Studies in Kappo (resuscitation methods) in Judo from the Viewpoint of Vaso-vagal Syndrome," Bulletin of the Association for the Scientific Studies on Judo, Report IV (Tokyo: Kodokan, 1972), 83.

forced into the lungs. Repeat until your victim wakes up.

Aggregate method (so-katsu)

The victim is lying on his back. You sit astride him near the victim's upper legs, with your left knee touching the mat and your right knee up in the air. Place both your palms (with the fingers spread and pointed towards his chest) below the navel (on the lower stomach). Push diagonally upward in the direction of the victim's chest with your hands and upper body. Repeat until the victim wakes up.

Back abdomen method (ura-katsu)

The victim is on his stomach with the face turned either to the right or the left. You sit astride the victim near his upper legs, with your left knee touching the mat and your right knee up in the air. Place both your palms just above the hips, and push diagonally upward in the direction of the victim's chest. Repeat until the victim wakes up.

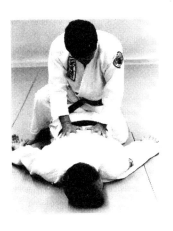 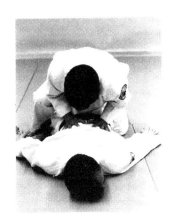

2. Testicle kappo (kogan-katsu)

This is designed to reduce the pain caused by kick to the testicles. Make the victim assume a sitting position, with his legs spread. Grasp him under the armpits from the rear. Lift the victim's body several inches off the mat. Drop his hips to the mat several times until his testicles become normal and the pain is reduced.

Another method is utilized when the victim is lying down on his back. Grasp the victim's foot, and hit his arch hard several times.

VII. Basic Techniques (kihon-waza)

Basic techniques are as follows: A. Thrusting and striking techniques, B. Kicking techniques, C. Blocking techniques, D. Joint techniques, and E. Throwing and choking techniques.

A. Thrusting and striking techniques (tsuki-to-uchi-waza)

Thrusting and striking techniques simulate the use of powerful weapons, because the power of the entire body and mind are focused in the fist, knife-hand, or elbow. With these, you may incapacitate your opponent by injuring bones, muscles, or internal organs. The essential goal of modern jujutsu, however, is to control the opponent without harm. Sometimes, we simply use the element of surprise against an opponent and follow up with another, such as joint techniques. Thrusting and striking techniques require speed, power, accuracy, and balance.

Thrusting and striking techniques are as follows: middle thrust (chudan-tsuki), upper thrust (jodan-tsuki), lower thrust (gedan-tsuki), palm-heel thrust (shotei-tsuki), crescent-hand thrust (mikazukite-tsuki), fist strike (ken-uchi), raising elbow strike (hiji-age-uchi), upper elbow strike (hiji-jodan-uchi), downward elbow strike (hiji-oroshi-uchi), back elbow strike (hiji-ushiro-uchi), upper knife-hand strike (shuto-jodan-uchi), downward knife-hand strike (shuto-oroshi-uchi), and horizontal knife-hand strike (shuto-suihei-uchi).

Key points

1. Release unnecessary tension from the shoulders, arms, and hands.

2. Keep in mind the shortest distance possible from the starting position of the fist to the target.

3. Power comes from the entire body, especially the hip movement.

4. Tense the abdominal muscles at the moment of contact with the target.

5. After stretching the arm, the fist is in front of the center of the body.

6. Exhale while attacking.

7. Keep your shoulders and body straight.

8. Simultaneously, pull the opposite fist toward the side of your chest as the thrusting fist moves out.

Middle thrust (chudan-tsuki)

For the middle thrust, assume the toes inward stance (haji-dachi). Stretch your left fist and arm out in front of your solar plexus (palm down). Bring your right fist towards the right side of your chest (palm up). This is your beginning position. Next, stretch your right arm straight towards the target, aiming the fist with full speed and power. Twist the right fist and arm 180 degrees counterclockwise before making contact with the target. Your right palm should be facing down at the time of contact. Simultaneously, your left fist withdraws towards the left side of your chest, the left fist and arm twisting 180 degrees counterclockwise before the fist reaches the left side of your chest. Your left palm should be facing up when the motion is completed. Do not move your shoulders forward or backward during the movement.

Next, repeat on the opposite side.

57

Upper thrust (jodan-tsuki)

Upper thrust involves the same movement as the middle thrust except that your fist is directed at your opponent's face.

Lower thrust (gedan-tsuki)

Lower thrust involves the same movement as the middle thrust except that your fist is directed at your opponent's groin.

Palm-heel thrust (shotei-tsuki)

A palm-heel thrust involves the same movement as upper thrust except that your hand is open and your palm-heel is directed at your opponent's chin. Bend the wrist outward to make the palm-heel.

Next, repeat on the opposite side.

Crescent-hand thrust (mikazukite-tsuki)

A crescent-hand thrust involves the same movement as upper thrust except that your hand is open and your crescent hand is directed at your opponent's neck. The striking part is the curved area between the index finger and the thumb.

Next, repeat on the opposite side.

Fist strike (ken-uchi)

Bring both your fists together in front of your chest. At this moment, bend your elbows to a 90 degree angle. Next, strike upward (face), sideways (stomach), sideways (face), or downward (groin) with your right fist. After the strike, bring your fist to the original position.

Next, repeat on the opposite side.

Raising elbow strike (hiji-age-uchi)

Bring your left fist to the side of your left ear with left elbow bent and pointed at your opponent. The right fist should be at the right side of your chest (palm up). Next, bring the right fist to the side of your right ear with your right elbow bent upward so that you can strike to the opponent's chin with your right elbow. At the same time, withdraw your left fist toward the left side of your chest (palm up).

Next, repeat on the opposite side.

Upper elbow strike (hiji-jodan-uchi)

Bring your left fist to the front of the left side of your chest (palm down) with your left elbow bent and upward. The right fist should be at the right side of your chest (palm up). Next, bring your right fist to the front of the right side of your chest with your right elbow bent. Then, strike the left side of his face from the right to the left with your right elbow. At the same time, withdraw your left fist toward the left side of your chest (palm up). (Or, strike middle of the body.)

Next, repeat on the opposite side.

Downward elbow strike (hiji-oroshi-uchi)

Bring your left fist to the front of the right side of your chest (palm down) with your left elbow bent. Bring your right fist to the back of your head with your right elbow bent upward. Next, strike straight downward with your right elbow. Simultaneously, withdraw your left fist toward the left side of your chest. Next, repeat on the opposite side.

Back elbow strike (hiji-ushiro-uchi)

Stretch your left arm out in front of your solar plexus (palm down). Bring your right fist towards the right side of your chest (palm up). Next, withdraw your left elbow straight backward until your fist reaches the side of your left chest (palm up). This will enable you to strike the target behind you with your left elbow. At the same time, stretch your right arm out in front of your solar plexus (palm down).

Next, repeat on the opposite side.

Upper knife-hand strike (shuto-jodan-uchi)

Bring your right knife-hand toward the side of your right ear, turning your palm up. The left hand is in front of your right chest with your left elbow bent (palm down). Next, strike the left side of your opponent's face from the right to the left with your right knife-hand (palm up), your arm bending slightly inward and your wrist bending outward at this moment. Simultaneously, withdraw your left hand toward the left side of your chest (palm up). Next, repeat on the opposite side.

Downward knife-hand strike (shuto-oroshi-uchi)

Bring your right knife-hand toward the top of your head. The left knife-hand is in front of your right chest (palm down) with your left elbow bent. Next, strike your opponent's left collarbone with your right knife-hand. Simultaneously, withdraw your left hand toward the left side of your chest (palm up).

Next, repeat on the opposite side.

Horizontal knife-hand strike (shuto-suihei-uchi)

Bring your right knife-hand toward the left side of your ear with your right elbow bent (palm down). At this moment, your right arm is on top of your left arm. Left hand should be in front of the right side of your chest (palm down). Next, strike his neck with your right knife-hand. At the same time, withdraw your left hand toward the left side of your chest (palm up).

Next, repeat on the opposite side.

B. Kicking techniques (keri-waza)

There are many kicking techniques, but in jujutsu, the most effective, powerful, and simple methods of kicking are used. The most important point of the kick is its degree of power.

Kicking techniques are as follows: knee kick (hiza-geri), front kick (mae-geri), side kick (yoko-geri), back kick (ushiro-geri), and round kick (mawashi-geri).

Key points

1. The knee of the supporting leg is slightly bent.

2. The supporting leg must maintain balance at all times while delivering the kick.

3. The knee of kicking leg must be straightened fully when the foot has reached its target.

4. After delivering the kick, immediately withdraw your leg to its original position to prevent the opponent from grabbing it and to prepare for the next attack.

Knee kick (hiza-geri)

The knee kick is delivered to the groin, abdomen, and face. It is used during close-distance fighting.

Assume a natural stance. Bend your left knee, and, at the same time, kick upward as hard and as high as you can with the kneecap.

Next, practice with the opposite knee.

Front kick (mae-geri)

The front kick is delivered to the shins, groin, abdomen, chest, and face.

Assume a natural stance. Bend your left knee, bringing your left foot to knee height, and kick forward in a straight line as hard as you can. Strike your target with the ball of your foot. Withdraw your left leg immediately to its original position.

Next, practice with the opposite leg.

Side kick (yoko-geri)

The side kick is delivered to the knee joints, shins, abdomen, and face when the opponent is alongside or in front of you.

Assume a natural stance. Bend your left knee, raising your left foot alongside of your right foot to knee level. Then kick to your left, snapping your leg out straight and striking your target with the outer edge of your foot. Withdraw your leg immediately to its original position.

Next, practice with the opposite leg.

Back kick (ushiro-geri)

The back kick is delivered to the abdomen, groin, face, and shins when your opponent is behind you.

Assume a natural stance. Bend your left knee, bringing your left foot to knee height. Then kick straight back with the sole of your foot. Contact should be made with the heel to your opponent's abdomen.

Next, practice with the opposite leg.

Round kick (mawashi-geri)

The round kick is delivered to the abdomen, kidneys, and face.

Assume a natural stance. Bend your left knee, and elevate your bent leg sideways, parallel to the ground; then deliver a kick forward. Pivot on the ball of your right foot, and twist your hips to reach your target. When aiming for the face, bend to your right to get proper elevation, bringing your leg up diagonally from the ground. Contact is made with the ball of your foot. Pull your leg back immediately to its original position.

Next, practice with the opposite leg.

C. Blocking techniques (uke-waza)

There are six basic blocking techniques: upper block (jodan-uke), middle outside block (chudan-soto-uke), middle inside block (chudan-uchi-uke), hook block (kake-uke), lower block (gedan-uke), and cross block (juji-uke).

Key points

1. The blocking arm makes contact with the target nearer to the elbow than to the wrist.

2. The blocking arm moves in a circular path.

3. The direction of your opponent's attack must be determined before blocking.

4. Use the block to change the direction of your opponent's attack rather than to stop it.

5. Maintain a flexible stance so that a counterattack can easily be implemented.

Upper block (jodan-uke)

The upper block is an effective defense against your opponent's kick or punch to the face or head.

The starting position is standing with your bent left arm on a level slightly higher than your forehead to protect your face. There should be a distance equal to two fists between forehead and forearm. Your right fist is held close to the right side of your chest. Next, bring your right arm up diagonally past your forehead, turning your fist and forearm away from your face. Simultaneously, lower your left fist to the left side of your chest. Blocking should be done with power and speed.

Practice on the opposite side.

Middle outside block (chudan-soto-uke)

The middle outside block is an effective defense against your opponent's attacking foot or hand in the area from below the shoulder down to the abdomen.

The starting position is standing with your right arm bent and your right fist alongside your head. The left arm is bent with the left fist in front of the right side of the chest (palm down). Next, swing your right arm across the front of your chest in a semicircle until your right fist is in front of your left shoulder (palm toward you). Your right arm is now extended about 120 degrees. At the same time, your left fist is pulled to the left side of your chest (palm up). Practice on the opposite side.

Middle inside block (chudan-uchi-uke)

The middle inside block is an effective defense against your opponent's punch to the midsection of the body.

The starting position is standing with your right arm bent and your right fist under your left armpit (palm down). The left arm is on top of the right arm, and your left fist is on your upper right arm (palm down). Next, swing your right arm across the front of your chest in a semicircle from the left to the right until your right fist is in front of your right shoulder (palm toward you). Your right arm is now extended about 120 degrees. Simultaneously, withdraw your left fist to the left side of your chest (palm up). Practice on the opposite side.

74

Hook block (kake-uke)

The hook block is an effective defense against your opponent's punch to the face.

The starting position is standing with your left arm bent and your left fist under your right armpit (palm down). The right arm is on top of the left arm, and your right fist is on your upper left arm (palm down). Next, swing your left arm across the front of your chest in a semicircle from the right to the left until your left open-hand is in front of your left shoulder (palm toward outside). Your left arm is now extended about 120 degrees. Simultaneously, withdraw your right fist to the right side of your chest (palm up). Practice on the opposite side.

Lower block (gedan-uke)

The lower block is used against the opponent's attacking foot or fist in the area of your lower abdomen or the lower part of the body.

The starting position is standing with your left arm bent and your left fist alongside the right side of the head. The right arm is extended in front of you with your right fist in front of your left thigh. Next, swing your left arm downward until the left fist is in front of the left thigh, making a 45 degree angle with your body. At the same time, your right arm is bent until the right fist is alongside the right side of your chest (palm up).

Cross block (juji-uke)

The cross block is used against attacks to the lower part of the body or to the head.

The starting position is standing in natural stance with your arms bent in front of your chest, wrists crossed, and fists tight (palms out). Next, extend your crossed wrists upward or downward against the attacking limb.

D. Joint techniques (kansetsu-waza)

Joint techniques involve attacking the physiologically weak points of the joint. The attacks are hitting, bending, stretching, and twisting. These are applied to the neck, shoulder, hip, spine, knee, ankle, toes, elbow, wrist, and finger. For example, the wrist joint can be attacked by bending the hand forward or backward, twisting it inward (toward the body) or outward (away from the body), or bending it to the right or to the left. This should be accomplished by using minimum power until your opponent feels pain. Further application of power will result in dislocation of the joint or damage to ligaments and bone.

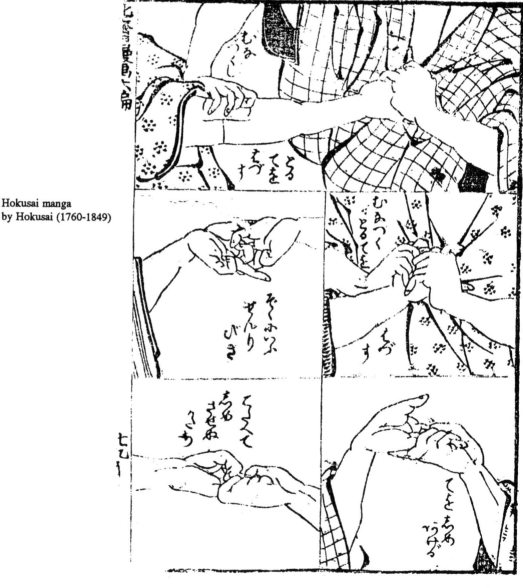

Hokusai manga
by Hokusai (1760-1849)

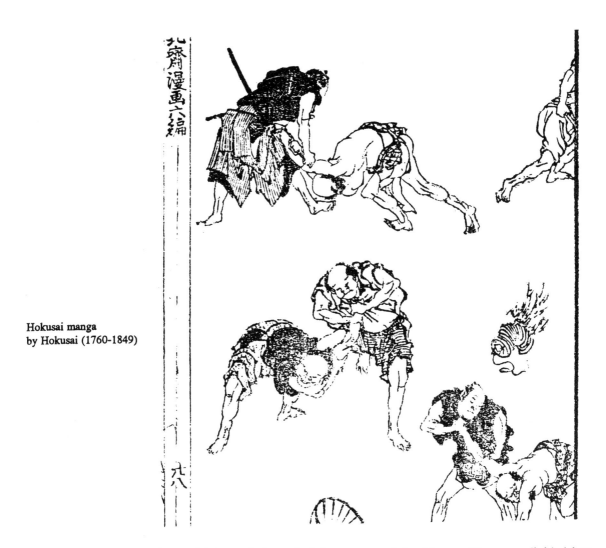

Hokusai manga
by Hokusai (1760-1849)

The most commonly used joint techniques in jujutsu are explained here. These are divided into three classes: 1. Wrist joint (tekubi-kansetsu), 2. Elbow joint (hiji-kansetsu), and 3. Neck joint (kubi-kansetsu).

Key points

1. Force your opponent off balance so that you need to use only a minimum amount of strength. For example: a) In applying hiji-gatame (elbow hold), spread your opponent's arm from his body at an angle greater than 90 degrees before applying pressure. When this limiting angle is reached, the arm is useless. b) In applying ude-hineri (twisting elbow to the inside), raise your opponent's elbow higher than his shoulder.

2. Use the element of surprise first; then apply a joint technique. For example, throw a punch first, then apply the technique.

Safety rules

There are dangers involved when practicing joint techniques. Therefore, safety rules must be followed.

1. When applying the joint technique, control your own power at all times in order to prevent damage to your opponent's joint. For example, when applying pressure to, or twisting or stretching a joint, do so gradually and slowly until your opponent feels a slight pain. Then, release immediately.

2. When the joint technique is applied and the opponent feels pain and is immobilized, a signal must be given. For example, when pain is felt, you must say, "I give up," or tap your opponent lightly several times so that he will release you from the joint technique.

1. Wrist joint (tekubi-kansetsu)

Twisting the wrist inward (kote-hineri)
Method I

Grasp your opponent's right hand by placing your right thumb at the base of his index finger. Tightly grip the back of his hand by wrapping your fingers around the heel of his palm. Next, twist your opponent's wrist clockwise in a circular motion until the joint is locked and the body starts to follow the motion.

Practice on the opposite side.

Method II

Grasp the back of your opponent's right hand with your right hand. At this time, your right palm is on top of the back of his four fingers. Next, twist your opponent's right hand clockwise with your right hand and bring his right hand in front of your face. Thus, you lock his right wrist joint.

Practice on the opposite side.

Twisting the wrist outward (kote-gaeshi)

Method I

Grasp your opponent's right hand with your left hand by placing your left thumb at the base of his little finger. Tightly grip his hand by wrapping your fingers around the ball of his thumb. Next, twist your opponent's wrist counterclockwise in a circular motion until the joint is locked.

Practice on the opposite side.

Method II

Your opponent's right hand is facing up (palm up). Grasp your opponent's right hand with your right hand by placing your right thumb at the base of his little finger from underneath. Tightly grip his hand by wrapping your fingers around the base of his thumb. At this time, your right palm is under the back of his four fingers. Next, twist your opponent's wrist counterclockwise in a circular motion until the joint is locked. Practice on the opposite side.

2. Elbow joint (hiji-kansetsu)

Elbow hold (hiji-gatame)

Grasp your opponent's right wrist first with your left hand from above (palm down), then follow with your right hand from underneath (palm up). Bring his right wrist to the right side of your chest with both your hands. Next, clamp the arm under your left arm. At this point, your opponent's arm should be held with the outside surface of his elbow facing upward. Next, advance your right foot diagonally to the right so that your opponent's arm is separated from his body at an angle greater than 90 degrees. Now, lift his right wrist, and press your left elbow into your opponent's elbow (outside surface).

Practice on the opposite side.

Twisting elbow to the inside (ude-hineri)

Grasp your opponent's right wrist strongly with both your hands from the outside (right hand from above and left hand from underneath). Bend his arm 90 degrees, keeping his right forearm parallel to the right side of his body. Push his elbow upward until it is slightly higher than his shoulder level. Next, advance your right foot to your opponent's right side, and pass underneath his right armpit. Turn your body counterclockwise 180 degrees. Then, twist your opponent's arm inward until he feels pain.

Practice on the opposite side.

Twisting elbow to the outside (ude-gaeshi)

Method 1

Grasp your opponent's right wrist from the outside with your right hand (four fingers on top). Next, bring your left arm to the top of his right inner elbow. Then, bring his right wrist up in front of your face with your right hand. Next, insert your left hand between your right forearm and his right forearm from above his right forearm. Bring his right wrist up in front of your face, and push his right wrist backward with your left knife-hand and right hand. Next, twist his right arm outward until he feels pain or falls down.

Practice on the opposite side.

Method 2

Grasp his right wrist from the inside with both your hands (left hand from above, right hand from underneath). Bring his right wrist in front of your head with both your hands. Advance your left foot diagonally to the right. Next, turn your body 180 degrees to the right. (At this moment your opponent's right arm is on top of your right shoulder.) Bring his right wrist downward with both your hands until he feels pain or falls down.

Practice on the opposite side.

3. Neck joint (kubi-kansetsu)

When practicing neck joint techniques, which are extremely dangerous to your opponent, you must control your own power and not use force when your target is reached. You must reduce speed and stop about one inch in front of your target.

Chin press (ago-oshi)

Strike your opponent's chin with the right (or left) heel of your palm from below his chin, diagonally up and backward. This will cause your opponent's neck to be damaged or completely broken.

Neck press (kubi-tsuki-age)

Strike your opponent's neck with your crescent-hand (mikazukite) from below, diagonally up and forward, thereby pushing him backward.

E. Throwing and choking techniques (nage-to-shime-waza)

I have selected those techniques which are the most effective for common use in jujutsu. Throwing and choking techniques are as follows: Big outside reaping (o-soto-gari), big hip throw (o-goshi), Forward foot sweep (de-ashi-harai), one-arm shoulder throw (ippon-seoi-nage), big inside reaping (o-uchi-gari), hip wheel (koshi-guruma), circle throw (tomoe-nage), shoulder wheel (kata-guruma), naked choke (hadaka-jime), and half-cross choke (kata-juji-jime).

Key points

1. Force your opponent off-balance, prepare to attack, and apply the techniques.

2. These movements are almost simultaneous (like one movement).

3. Know the direction of your opponent's power and movements.

4. Your center of gravity should always be lower than your opponent's.

5. Apply the techniques with good timing and movement.

6. Initiate your attack from a distance.

7. Assuming natural position, bend your knees slightly when you meet your opponent.

8. Repeat one technique continuously.

Hokusai manga
by Hokusai (1760-1849)

Big outside reaping (o-soto-gari)

O-soto-gari is most useful against attacks involving middle and upper thrusts. This applies to both close and distance fighting.

You are in the right foot forward stance facing your opponent, who is also in the right foot forward stance. Grasp each other's left upper lapels with the right hand. Then, grasp the outside of each other's right sleeves near the elbow with the left hand. Next, step forward alongside your opponent's right foot with your left foot. Simultaneously, pull his sleeve with your left hand to your left, and with your right hand push your opponent's left upper chest backward so that your opponent loses balance to your left front corner. Next, your right leg moves forward until it is past your opponent's right leg.

Then, swing your right leg backward, sweeping the back of your opponent's right kneecap upward with the back of your right kneecap. This will enable you to throw your unbalanced opponent.

Practice on the left side.

Big hip throw (o-goshi)

This technique may be applied against close front techniques, especially body grabbing.

You are in the right foot forward stance facing your opponent, who is also in the natural stance. Grasp each other's left upper lapels with the right hand. Then, grasp the outside of each other's right sleeves near the elbow with the left hand. Pull your opponent with your left hand so that your opponent's balance is broken to his front. At the same time, your right foot advances to a position in front of your opponent's right foot. Pivot on this foot so that your toes are pointing in the same direction as your opponent's toes (about 12 inches in front of your opponent's right foot). Next, bend your right knee, and lower your body. Release your grip with the right hand, and slide your right arm under your opponent's left armpit until you reach the right side of your opponent's waist. Then, tighten your arm around his body. Turn your body to the left and draw your left foot into position in front of your opponent's left foot. Your opponent's and your toes should be pointing in the same direction. The distance between your feet should be about your own shoulder-width. Bend your knees, keeping your back straight and in close contact with the front of your opponent's body.

Move your hips a little to the right; then straighten your knees, and bend your upper body forward, simultaneously pulling forcefully with both your hands so that your opponent is thrown forward over your right hip.

Practice on the left side.

Forward foot sweep (de-ashi-harai)

This technique may be applied when your opponent has advanced into a fighting stance or when your opponent has attempted a front kick and you have grasped his leg.

You and your opponent face each other in the natural stance. Grasp each other's left upper lapels with the right hand. Then, grasp the outside of each other's right sleeves near the elbow with the left hand. When your opponent takes a step forward on his right foot (or if he is already in advanced position) and as his weight is changing from the rear foot to the front foot, sweep your opponent's right foot diagonally from the left to the right. The sole of your left foot is applied to the outside portion of your opponent's heel and ankle. The sweep is delivered while pulling down with your left hand and pushing with your right hand so that your opponent is thrown in front of you. Practice on the left side.

One-arm shoulder throw (ippon-seoi-nage)

This technique supplies a defense against middle and upper thrusts, strikes from the front, or body attacks from the rear.

You are in the right foot forward stance facing your opponent, who is also in the natural stance. Grasp each other's left upper lapels with the right hand. Then, grasp the outside of each other's right sleeves near the elbow with the left hand. Pull your opponent with your left hand (your opponent's balance is broken to his right front), and simultaneously advance your right foot to a position in front of your opponent's right foot. Pivot so that your toes are pointing in the same direction as your opponent's toes (about 12 inches in front of your opponent's right foot). Next, bending your right knee, lower your body, release your right hand, and thrust your right arm under your opponent's right armpit, bending your right elbow tightly. Then, turn to the left, drawing your left foot in front of your opponent's left foot (toes pointing in the same direction as his). Your back should be in close contact with your opponent's body. Your feet should be shoulder-width apart with both knees bent.

Next, straighten your knees, and bend your upper body forward, pulling with both your hands. This causes your opponent to be thrown forward over your right shoulder.

Practice on the left side.

Big inside reaping (o-uchi-gari)

This technique supplies a defense against your opponent's front kick, side kick, and round kick.

You and your opponent face each other in the natural stance. Grasp each other's left upper lapels with the right hand. Then, grasp the outside of each other's right sleeves near the elbow with the left hand. With your left foot step forward toward the inside of your opponent's right foot. Simultaneously, push the left side of your opponent's chest with your right hand. This unbalance him to his left rear corner. Next, advance your right foot forward between your opponent's feet, and sweep his left foot from the left to the right in a half circle with your heel leading the movement. At this time, the back of your right knee will be in contact with the back of your opponent's left knee, which will cause your opponent to fall backward.

Practice on the left side.

Hip wheel (koshi-guruma)

This defense technique may be applied against punches and round kick.

You are in the right foot forward stance facing your opponent, who is also in the natural stance. Grasp each other's left upper lapels with the right hand. Then, grasp the outside of each other's right sleeves near the elbow with the left hand. Now break your opponent's balance forward by pulling with your left hand. At the same time, advance your right foot to a position in front of your opponent's right foot. Pivot so that your toes are pointing in the same direction as your opponent's toes (about 12 inches from your opponent's right foot). Next, bend your right knee, lower your body, release your grip with the right hand, and encircle your opponent's neck tightly with your right arm. Next, turn your body to the left, moving your left foot in front of your opponent's left foot. Your toes are now pointing in the same direction as your opponent's toes. Your feet are shoulder-width apart, and the knees are bent. Your back is in close contact with the front of your opponent's body. Thrust your hips deeply to the right, past your opponent's right hip.

Them, straighten your knees, and twist your upper body forward and to the left, pulling forcefully with your left hand and right arm. This will cause your opponent to be thrown forward over your right hip.

Practice on the left side.

Circle throw (tomoe-nage)

This technique may be applied against close-front techniques, especially choking from the front.

You and your opponent face each other in the natural stance. Grasp each other's left upper lapels with the right hand. Then, grasp the outside of each other's right sleeves near the elbow with the left hand. Pull your opponent toward you with both your hands (lifting-pull). Simultaneously, advance your left foot deeply (bending the knee slightly) between your opponent's legs so that your opponent is forced off-balance to his front. Bend your right leg, and place the sole of your right foot below your opponent's navel.

Next, drop your hips near your left heel, and lie down on the mat. Pull your opponent with both your hands as you push his body up with your right foot so that your opponent falls over your head.

Practice on the left side.

Shoulder wheel (kata-guruma)

This advanced technique may be applied against close-front techniques and far distance upper thrust.

You are in the right foot forward stance facing your opponent, who is also in the natural stance. Grasp each other's left upper lapels with the right hand. Then, grasp the outside of each other's right sleeves near the elbow with the left hand. Pull your opponent with your left hand so that your opponent's balance is broken to his right front corner. Advance your right foot forward between your opponent's legs to a position behind his feet, and release your right hand from his lapel; bend both your knees deeply, and insert your right arm. Grasp his right upper leg tightly with your right hand and arm, pressing the right side of your head and shoulder to the right side of his lower stomach.

Pull his right sleeve straight toward your left side with your left hand. Simultaneously, stand up so that you carry him up on both your shoulders. Next, pull his right sleeve (or right arm) toward your chest with your left hand, and push his right leg up with your right arm and right shoulder. He will then fall down on his back.

Practice on the left side.

Naked choke (hadaka-jime)

Apply this technique whenever you find yourself behind your opponent. For example: Your opponent attacks with his fist or with a kick. You block and step behind him to apply this technique.

Stand behind your opponent, pass your right forearm in front of your opponent's throat, and position the middle (inner side) of your forearm against your opponent's throat. Grasp your left hand with your right hand near your opponent's left shoulder. Then press your opponent's head firmly with your right shoulder, and pull straight toward your chest with both your arms so that you can choke him.

Half cross choke (kata-juji-jime)

When your opponent is in front of you or when you have thrown him and he is lying down facing you, you may apply this technique.

Stand in front of your opponent. Grasp your opponent's lapel on the left side, near the left side of his collarbone with your left hand (the palm toward you, the fingers inside). Grasp your opponent's right lapel near the right side of his neck with your right hand (the palm toward your opponent, the fingers outside). Pull his left lapel with your left hand, and push to the right side of his neck with your right hand and forearm so that you can choke him.

VIII. Jujutsu Techniques (jujutsu-no-waza)

The techniques of modern jujutsu include nearly two thousand different movements, and up until the present, these numerous techniques have not been classified in any way. I have investigated these techniques and have developed a system of classification for the benefit of the teacher and student of jujutsu.

To develop effective jujutsu techniques, you need speed, power, accuracy, and balance, as well as counterattacks using well-controlled movements. Also required are proper stances and the maintenance of proper distance, eye contact, and judgment.

Classifications are as follows: A. Chikama-no-waza (close-front techniques), B. Yoko-no-waza (side techniques), C. Ushiro-no-waza (rear techniques), D. Tohma-no-waza (far-front techniques), E. Suwari-waza (kneeling techniques), F. Tanto-ni-taisuru-waza (against knife techniques), G. Bo-ni-taisuru-waza (against staff techniques), H. Yari-ni-taisuru-waza (against spear techniques), I. Katana-ni-taisuru-waza (against sword techniques), J. Tanju-ni-taisuru-waza (against pistol techniques), and K. Kumi-tachi (sword against sword techniques).

The progression of jujutsu techniques is such that the easiest and most effective methods of defense are found in method I. The moderately difficult are found in method II. Beyond that are the more advanced techniques.

Key points

1) You must apply the techniques before your opponent completes his hold on you.

2) You must discover the direction of your opponent's attack in order to avoid the power of his movement.

3) Proper use of the mind enables the body to respond naturally.

4) Maintain a flexible stance.

5) Exhibit split-second judgment and timing.

6) Know which weapon will be used.

7) Deduce your opponent's intent by the movement of his eyes.

Safety rules

There are dangers involved when practicing jujutsu without rules, so you must follow the safety rules.

1) When applying joint techniques, control your power. For example, if you hold the back of your opponent's elbow joint completely, do not increase your power. Instead, reduce your power, and slowly press until the opponent feels a slight pain so that he may signal submission by tapping his hand on your body lightly several times (this signal applies to choking techniques too), or he must say, "I give up." When you receive a give up signal, you must release your opponent from joint or choking techniques.

2) Your hand or foot must be stopped two inches in front of the target area of your opponent's body when applying punching or kicking techniques.

A. Chikama-no-waza (close-front techniques)

Chikama-no-waza (close-front techniques) are defenses against seizure from the front. You and your opponent are always within reaching distance, which means that your opponent can hit you without changing his position. Keep your eyes on your opponent's entire body, relax your body, and stand naturally so that you can react very fast.

The classifications of chikama-no-waza are as follows: 1. Mae-kubi-jime (front strangle), 2. Mae-kumi-tsuki (front body seizure), 3. Mae-katate-dori (front single-hand seizure), 4. Mae-ryote-dori (front double-hand seizure), and 5. Mae-eri-dori (front lapel seizure).

1. Mae-kubi-jime (front strangle)

Method I

Your opponent is choking you from the front with both his hands. Form a triangle with your hands and elbows, and push both your hands up in between your opponent's arms (so that you can release your opponent's choke).

Next, grab both your opponent's arms, and pull him forward while kicking him in the groin.

Method II

Your opponent is choking you from the front with both his hands. Move your right foot diagonally behind your left foot, and raise your left hand over his right arm in a circular motion towards your right side so that you can release his choke. Next, hit your opponent's face with your left knife-hand (shuto).

Method III

Your opponent is choking you from the front with both his hands. Move your left foot backward so that your opponent is forced off-balance. At the same time, break your opponent's left elbow by hitting it forcefully with your right forearm. Then, with the same hand strike your opponent's face.

Method IV

Your opponent is choking you from the front with both his hands. Grasp both of your opponent's arms, and apply tomoe-nage (circle throw).

Method V

Your opponent is standing in front of you and grasps your left and right lapels with his left and right hands respectively. Your opponent crosses his arms under your chin with his left forearm above the right and then attempts to choke you. Step backward with you left foot, and hit your opponent's face with your right fist. Next, insert your left knife-hand (shuto) between your opponent's forearms. Pass your left forearm, with your fingers pointing upward, in front of your face. At this point, your left elbow is on your opponent's right forearm. Immediately, press down with your left elbow so that you can release your opponent's choke.

Next, grasp your opponent's left wrist with your left hand (thumb down), and pull towards the left side of your chest. Next, grasp your opponent's left elbow with your right hand (thumb down). While pushing up toward his right side with your right hand and twisting counterclockwise with your left hand, step diagonally with your right foot toward your left side so that your opponent falls down with the right falling forward with roll-out (migi-zenpo-kaiten-ukemi).

2. Mae-kumi-tsuki (front body seizure)

Mae-kumi-tsuki (front body seizure) has two classifications: 1) Mae-uchi-kumi-tsuki (front under arm body seizure), 2) Mae-soto-kumi-tsuki (front over arm body seizure).

1). Mae-uchi-kumi-tsuki (front under arm body seizure).

Method I

Your opponent is grasping your body under the arms from the front. You can open both hands and hit your opponent's ears, or kick your opponent's groin with your right knee.

Method II

Your opponent is grasping your body under the arms from the front. Thrust to your opponent's eyes with your fingers.

Method III

Your opponent is grasping your body under the arms from the front. Strike his chin with your left palm-heel (shotei). Next, grasp his chin with your left hand and grasp the hair on the back of his head with your right hand. Twist his neck clockwise until he falls down on the mat. Then, twist his neck until he gives up.

2) Mae-soto-kumi-tsuki (front over arm body seizure)

Method I

Your opponent is grasping your body over the arms from the front. You kick his groin with your right knee or left knee.

Method II

Your opponent is grasping your body over the arms from the front. Grasp his body with both your arms. Kick your opponent's groin with your right knee. Next, advance your right foot forward between his feet, and sweep the back of your opponent's left knee toward you from the left to the right with the back of your right knee so that he falls down on his back. At this time, you fall down on his stomach.

Method III

Your opponent is grasping your body over the arms from the front. Kick your opponent's groin with your right knee, and apply right o-goshi (big hip throw).

3. Mae-katate-dori (front single-hand seizure)

Mae-katate-dori (front single-hand seizure) has two classifications: 1) Mae-ai-katate-dori (front cross single-hand seizure), 2) Mae-gyaku-katate-dori (front straight single-hand seizure).

1) Mae-ai-katate-dori (front cross single-hand seizure)

Method I

Your opponent is grasping your right wrist with his right hand. Thrust the right side of his face with your left fist.

Method II

Your opponent is grasping your right wrist with his right hand. Advance your left foot behind your opponent's right foot. Simultaneously, strike his neck with your left knife-hand (palm down). Next, grasp and pull his neck toward you from the right to the left with your left hand so that his hip joint is taken by your left upper leg and left arm. Then, hit his groin with your right knife-hand. Your opponent falls down on his back.

Method III

Your opponent is grasping your right wrist with his right hand. Bend your right elbow downward, with the fingers of your right hand pointing straight up (at this time, your right hand is outside of his right wrist); simultaneously bend your knees. Next, grab your opponent's wrist with your right hand from above, and twist your right hand clockwise (so your opponent is forced off-balance). Then, grasp his right elbow with your left hand (thumb down). Push up with your left hand, and twist with your right hand. At the same time, step forward with your left foot so that your opponent falls down on his back with a left zenpo-kaiten-ukemi (falling forward with roll-out).

Method IV

Your opponent is grasping your right wrist with his right hand. Hold his right hand tightly against your right wrist with your left hand. Next, rotate your right hand from the left to the right, and bring it upward in a circular motion so that your right hand is on top of his right wrist. At this time, your opponent's right knife-hand is facing up, and in front of your right side. Push down on the knife-hand side of his wrist with your right hand (palm down). You control his right wrist with your hands, causing him to bend his knees.

Release your right hand slightly so that he is trying to stand up. At this moment, advance your right foot and thrust to his neck with your right crescent-hand (mikazukite). Your opponent falls down on his back.

Method V

Your opponent is grasping your right wrist with both his hands. Simultaneously, bend your right elbow downward with the fingers of your right hand pointing straight up, and bend your knees. Next, thrust your right fingertips (palm inward) into his face so that he falls down on his back.

Method VI

Your opponent is grasping your right wrist with both his hands. Advance your left foot behind his right foot. Strike his neck with your left knife-hand.

At the same time, grasp the left side of his neck and push backward with your left forearm so that he falls down on his back. Then, kick his body with your left heel.

123

Method VII

Your opponent is grasping your right wrist with both his hands. Next, bend your right elbow outward with the fingers of your right hand pointing straight up, and bring it up in front of your face. Simultaneously, turn your body 90 degrees to the left. Therefore, your opponent is off-balanced diagonally forward. Advance your right foot and bring your right hand diagonally downward (palm down) so that your opponent falls down on his back with a right zenpo-kaiten-ukemi.

124

2) Mae-gyaku-katate-dori (front straight single-hand)

Method I

Your opponent is grasping your left wrist with his right hand. Kick your opponent's groin with your right (or left) knee or hit his face with your free hand. Next, push his chin with your right palm-heel so that your opponent falls down on his back.

Method II

Your opponent is grasping your left wrist with his right hand. Grasp your opponent's right wrist with your right hand (thumb up). Next, pull your opponent's right arm up with both your hands in front of the right side of your face. Advance your left foot diagonally to the right so that it passes just behind your right foot. Turn your body 270 degrees towards the right, and bring his right hand to the right side of your face with both your hands; then pull your opponent's right wrist with both your hands so that your opponent falls down on his back. If your opponent will not fall, his right elbow will be dislocated.

126

Method III

Your opponent is grasping your left wrist with his right hand. You bring your left hand to in front of your stomach (palm up). Grasp your opponent's right hand from underneath with your right hand (palm up), and his right hand from above with your left hand (palm down). Withdraw your left foot diagonally towards your right back corner while turning your body to the left. Twist his right hand counterclockwise with both your hands, and pull his hand toward your chest so that he falls down on his back (zenpo-kaiten-ukemi).

Your opponent is grasping your upper left arm with his right hand and trying to hit you in the face with his left hand. Move your right foot diagonally behind your left foot (so you can avoid his fist). Raise your left hand over his right arm in a circular motion towards your right side so that you can release his grip. Next, hit your opponent's face with your left knife-hand.

Method V

Your opponent is grasping your upper left arm with his right hand and trying to hit you in the face with his left hand. Move your right foot diagonally behind your left foot. Hold his right hand tightly against your left upper arm with your right hand. Next, bring your left arm up from the left to the right with a circular motion so that your left forearm is above his right wrist. At this time, his right knife-hand is facing up. Push down on the knife-hand side of his wrist with your left forearm until your opponent falls down on his stomach. You can take your opponent's right wrist joint.

129

4. Mae-ryote-dori (front double-hand seizure)

Method I

Your opponent is grasping both your wrists (or arms) with both his hands. Then, withdraw both your hands backward to break your opponent's balance forward, and kick to his groin with your right (or left) knee.

Method II

Your opponent is grasping both your wrists and is trying to kick you in the groin with his knee. Simultaneously, withdraw your left foot diagonally to the left rear, and raise both your hands to the left side. Next, bend your right hand inward with your right elbow outward so that you can break your opponent's hold. Then, strike your opponent's face with your right hand.

Next, grasp his right wrist with your left hand, and bring it to the right side of your chest. At this time, grasp your opponent's right wrist with your right hand from underneath. Withdraw your right foot to the rear while pressing the back of your opponent's right elbow under your left arm so that you can control your opponent's right arm (hiji-gatame).

Method III

Your opponent is grasping both your wrists. Move both your hands to the center of your body until your hands are crossed. Grasp your opponent's right wrist with your right hand (thumb up). Next, hit your opponent's right elbow from the outside with your left arm. At the same time, step forward with your left foot. Immediately, pull your opponent's right arm up with both your hands, and turn your body 180 degrees towards the right; then, carry your opponent's right arm on your left shoulder.

Next, turn your body 180 degrees towards the right and pull your opponent's arm downward with both your hands so that your opponent falls down on his back.

Method IV

Your opponent is grasping both your wrists with both his hands. Advance your left foot diagonally to the left. Simultaneously, stretch your left hand diagonally downward (fingers straight). Immediately, stretch the fingers of your right hand upward, and push your right hand directly toward your opponent's face. (Your opponent should thus be forced off-balance to his right rear corner.) Advance your right foot to your opponent's right side, and place it behind his right foot. Keep pushing with both your hands so that your opponent falls down on his back.

Method V

Your opponent is grasping both your wrists with both his hands. Move both your hands to the center of your body until your hands are crossed (right hand above left hand; right palm up, left palm down). Next, grasp your opponent's right wrist with your right hand (palm up); then, strike his left elbow with your right arm and turn your body to the left. Next, grasp his right wrist with your left hand (palm down), and advance your right foot and push his left elbow with your right arm and bring his right hand in front of your face with both your hands. Next, push and pull his right wrist in a circle downward to your stomach with both your hands so that he falls down with a right zenpo-kaiten-ukemi.

Method VI

Your opponent is grasping both your wrists with both his hands. Move both your hands to the center of your body until your hands are crossed (left hand above right, with both palms up). Next, grasp your opponent's right hand from underneath with your right hand (palm up) and his right hand from above with your left hand (palm down). Withdraw your left foot diagonally towards your right back corner while turning your body to the left. Next, twist his right hand counterclockwise with both your hands, and pull his hand toward your stomach so that your opponent falls down on his back (zenpo-kaiten-ukemi).

5. Mae-eri-dori (front lapel seizure)

Method I

Your opponent is grasping your lapel with his right hand and is trying to hit your face with his other hand. Move your right foot diagonally to a position behind your left foot, and turn your body to the right. Next, hit his right elbow with your left forearm. Then, hit his neck with your left knife-hand.

Method II

Your opponent is grasping your lapel with his right hand and is trying to hit your face with his left hand. Move your right foot diagonally to a position behind your left foot, turning your body to the right (so that you can avoid his fist). Raise your left hand over his right arm in a circular motion towards your right side so that your opponent is forced off-balance. At this time, hit your opponent's face with your left knife-hand (shuto).

139

Your opponent is grasping your lapel with his right hand and pushing you. You grip the middle of your opponent's sleeve (or forearm) with your left hand and apply right ippon-seoi-nage (one-arm shoulder throw).

Method IV

Your opponent is grasping your lapel with his left hand and pushing you. You grasp his left wrist with your left hand. Withdraw your left foot diagonally to the right and turn your body 180 degrees, bringing your right arm under your opponent's elbow and moving upward while pulling your opponent's left wrist diagonally down to your left. This results in taking his left elbow and shoulder joint (right ippon-seoi-nage method). You must control, do not throw!

141

Method V

Your opponent is grasping your lapel with his right hand and is trying to hit you with his left hand. You quickly strike your opponent's face with your right fist before he hits you. Simultaneously, grasp your opponent's right hand with your left hand (place your left thumb at the middle of the back of your opponent's hand from the outside, four fingers gripped tightly over his palm). Next, grasp the opponent's right hand with your right hand: your right thumb is placed at the middle of the back of your opponent's hand, four fingers tightly gripped over his palm and the lapel of your own uniform (kote-gaeshi).

Next, move your left foot backward to the back of your right foot. Simultaneously, twist your opponent's wrist counterclockwise with both your hands so that your opponent falls down on his back. After you throw your opponent, hit his face with your right fist.

Method VI

Your opponent is grasping your lapel with his right hand and is trying to hit you with his left hand. Before your opponent is able to hit you, strike his face with your right fist. Then, grasp your opponent's right hand with your right hand from above (your right thumb should be placed at the base of the index finger, while the back of the opponent's hand is gripped tightly between your palm and the remaining fingers). Next, twist your opponent's right hand clockwise with your right hand (kote-hineri), grasp the back of your opponent's right elbow with your left hand (thumb down), and push upward with your left hand,

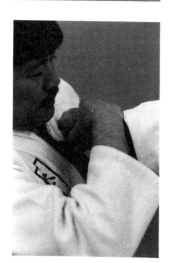

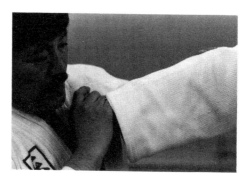

then, advance your left foot to a position between your right foot and his left foot, and advance your right foot so that your opponent falls down on his face. After your opponent is prone, press his right elbow and wrist to the mat with both your hands.

B. Yoko-no-waza (side techniques)

Yoko-no-waza (side techniques) are defenses against seizures from the side. The classifications of side techniques (yoko-no-waza) are as follows: 1. Yoko-kubi-jime (side strangle), 2. Yoko-kubi-kime (side neck lock), 3. Yoko-kumi-tsuki (side body seizure), and 4. Yoko-kataude-dori (side single-arm seizure).

1. Yoko-kubi-jime (side strangle)

Method I

Your opponent is trying to choke you from your right side with both his hands. Simultaneously, strike your opponent's eyes with the fingers of your left hand. Or, move your left foot to the left, and kick your opponent's knee joint with your right foot (side kick).

146

Method II

Your opponent is trying to choke you from your right side with both his hands. Simultaneously, move your entire body with your left foot leading to the left. Raise your right hand above your opponent's arms, and pull your right hand toward your left side so that your opponent is forced off-balance or releases you from the choke hold. Next, hit your opponent's face with your right knife-hand.

Method III

Your opponent is trying to choke you from your right side with both his hands. You move your left foot to the left, and hold his left hand tightly against your right shoulder with your left hand. Next, bring your right arm up from the right to the left with a circular motion so that your right forearm is above his left forearm. At this time, his left knife-hand is facing up. Push down on the knife-hand side of his left wrist with your right forearm until your opponent falls down on his stomach. Then, you can take your opponent's left wrist and elbow joint.

Method IV

Your opponent is trying to choke you from your right side with both his hands. Strike his groin with your right knife-hand. Grasp his right wrist with your left hand (thumb up) from underneath, and grasp his right elbow with your right hand (thumb up) from underneath. Advance your left foot diagonally to the right, and turn your body 90 degrees to the right. Pull his right elbow toward you with your right hand. Then, push his right hand and arm with your left shoulder so that his right wrist and elbow joint is taken by your hands and left shoulder.

Method V

Your opponent is trying to choke you from your right side with both his hands. Simultaneously, grasp your opponent's right forearm or sleeve with your left hand. Next, withdraw your left foot diagonally to the right so that it becomes parallel to your right foot (at this time, your feet should be shoulder-width apart), turn your body 90 degrees counterclockwise, and apply right ippon-seoi-nage (one-arm shoulder throw).

Method VI

Your opponent is trying to choke you from your right side with both his hands. Grasp the back of your opponent's right hand with your left hand from above (forefingers up). At the same time, strike his chin with your right fist. Next, grasp the back of his right hand with your right hand (forefingers up).

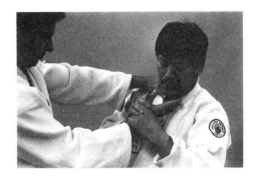

151

Twist his right hand counterclockwise with both your hands so that he falls down on his back. Strike his face with your right fist.

2. Yoko-kubi-kime (side neck lock)

Method I

Your opponent's left arm is around your neck and is trying to break your neck from your right side. Simultaneously, hit your opponent's groin with your left hand so that your opponent will loosen his hold. At this time push your opponent's arm and body with both your hands, and move backward with both your feet so that you can escape from his hold. Next, kick the back of his body with your right foot (front kick)

Method II

Your opponent's left arm is around your neck and is trying to break your neck from your right side. Simultaneously, strike your opponent's eyes with your left fingers. Next, put your right arm in front of your opponent's neck and across his body. At the same time, stretch out your right foot behind both of your opponent's legs. Drop your body backward, and push your right hand backward so that your opponent falls down on his back. After you and your opponent fall down, hit your opponent's groin, solar plexus, or face with your left fist.

Method III

Your opponent's left arm is around your neck and is trying to break your neck from your right side. Simultaneously, hit your opponent's groin with your left hand. Next, grasp your opponent's right arm with your left hand, and apply right o-goshi (big hip throw). After you throw your opponent, hit his face with your right fist.

3. Yoko-kumi-tsuki (side body seizure)

Method I

Your opponent is grasping your body over the arm from your right side. Simultaneously, hit your opponent's groin with your right hand (palm toward target), and raise your left hand straight upward so that you can release yourself from your opponent's hold. Next, strike your opponent's eyes with your left fingertips.

Method II

Your opponent is grasping your body over the arm from your right side. Simultaneously, grasp your opponent's right sleeve or forearm with your left hand, and hold his right upper arm with your right upper arm and forearm. Turn your body 90 degrees to the left and drop your right knee onto the mat (left knee in upright position). At this time, your right leg is in between his legs. Pull his right sleeve or forearm with your left hand and right arm. Immediately, bend your upper body forward so that he falls down on his back. Next, strike his face with your right hand.

Method III

Your opponent is grasping your body over the arm from your right side. Simultaneously, grasp your opponent's right arm with both your hands, and advance your right foot to a position just outside of his right foot with toes pointing in the same direction as his toes. Next, twist your upper body to the left, and throw your body counterclockwise so that your opponent falls down on his back. Next, strike his body with your left elbow.

Method IV

Your opponent is grasping your body over the arm from your right side. Simultaneously, hit your opponent's groin with your right knife-hand. Move your left foot to the left, and spread your left arm outside so that you can release his grasp. Next, hold his right wrist with your left forearm and upper arm, and his right forearm with your right forearm and upper arm. Turn your body 90 degrees to the right. Press his right wrist or forearm toward you with your left forearm and right forearm, and bend your upper body forward. You can take his wrist joint, or forearm.

4. Yoko-kataude-dori (side single-arm seizure)

Method I

Your opponent is grasping your right arm with both his hands from your right side (your upper arm is held by his left hand, and your wrist is held by his right hand). Advance your left foot, and kick your opponent's knee or groin with your right foot (side kick).

Method II

Your opponent is grasping your right arm with both his hands from your right side. Turn your body 90 degrees to the right and advance your left foot toward him. Next, thrust to his neck with your left crescent-hand (mikazuki-te). Then, with the same hand push him down.

Method III

Your opponent is grasping your right arm with both his hands from your right side. Turn your body 90 degrees to the left and withdraw your left foot diagonally to the right passing your right foot. Next, strike the back of his head with your left elbow. Release your right hand from his grasp. Move your right foot to the left passing in front of your left foot and turn your body 180 degrees to the left. You are now behind his back. Next, pass your right forearm in front of your opponent's throat, and position the middle of your forearm against his throat. Grasp your left hand with your right hand near his left shoulder. Press your opponent's head firmly with your right shoulder, and pull straight toward your chest with both your arms so that you can choke him.

Method IV

Your opponent is encircling your right arm with both his arms from your right side. Hit your opponent's face with your left fist. Then, turn your body 180 degrees clockwise. At the same time, grasp his neck with your left hand, and grasp his left arm with your right hand. Simultaneously, apply left o-soto-gari (big outside reaping).

C. Ushiro-no-waza (rear techniques)

Ushiro-no-waza (rear techniques) are defenses against being seized from the rear.

You have no eyes in the back of your head, so you must interpret your opponent's movement through the use of other senses. You may feel the movement of air signalling someone's presence. The opponent's footsteps, touch, or grasp will give you the necessary information concerning his movement. At this moment, you apply the technique.

The classifications of rear techniques (ushiro-no-waza) are as follows: 1. Ushiro-jime (rear strangle), 2. Ushiro-katate-dori (rear single-hand seizure), 3. Ushiro-ryote-dori (rear double-hand seizure), 4. Ushiro-eri-dori (rear collar seizure), 5. Ushiro-kumi-tsuki (rear body seizure), and 6. Ushiro-ryoude-kime (rear double-arm lock).

1. Ushiro-jime (rear strangle)

Method I

Your opponent is trying to choke you with both his hands from the rear. Immediately, advance your right foot diagonally to a position in front of your left foot, just a little to the left side, and turn your body 180 degrees counterclockwise. At the same time, grasp your opponent's left wrist with your left hand from the right to the left, and pull downward. Next, strike your opponent's kidney or face with your right hand.

Method II

Your opponent clasps his right arm around your neck and tries to choke you from the rear. Immediately, move your right foot and hip to the right side, and hit your opponent's groin with your left fist (palm toward your opponent). Then, escape from his choke.

Method III

Your opponent clasps his right arm around your neck and tries to choke you from the rear. Simultaneously, pull your chin in, and grasp your opponent's right forearm with both your hands (thumb toward you). Apply right ippon-seoi-nage (one-arm shoulder throw).

Method IV

Your opponent clasps his right arm around your neck and tries to choke you from the rear. Simultaneously, pull your chin in, grasp your opponent's right forearm with your left hand (thumb toward you), and grasp his right upper arm with your right hand. Immediately, pull downward on your opponent's right arm with both your hands. Then, twist your body 90 degrees clockwise, and apply right o-soto-gari (big outside reaping).

Method V

Your opponent clasps his right arm around your neck and tries to choke you from the rear. Simultaneously, pull your chin in, grasp your opponent's right forearm with both your hands (thumbs toward you), and immediately place his forearm on your chest, holding it there tightly. Bend your knees, and withdraw your left foot diagonally backward to a position between your right foot and your opponent's right foot. Turn your body 180 degrees counterclockwise to pass your body under his right armpit. Withdraw your left foot backward, and press (or snap) your opponent's right elbow with your right shoulder so that his elbow is locked (or broken) by your shoulder and hands.

Method VI

Your opponent clasps his right arm around your neck and tries to choke you from the rear. Simultaneously, pull your chin in, grasp your opponent's right forearm with both your hands (thumb toward you), and immediately place his forearm to your chest, holding it there tightly. Bend your knees, and withdraw your left foot diagonally backward to a position between your right foot and his right foot. Next, advance your right foot to a position between his right foot and your left foot, and drop your entire body as you twist counterclockwise so that your opponent falls down on his back.

Method VII

Your opponent holds your right arm with his right hand and is trying to choke you with his left forearm from the rear. Hit your opponent's left kidney with your left elbow. At the same time, stretch your right fingers and arm downward (so that you can release his hold). Grasp the back of his left hand with your right hand. Then, grasp his left wrist with your left hand. Next, stepping deeply, move your right foot backward to a position between your left foot and his left foot. Pass your body under your opponent's left armpit. Next, using both your hands, push his left elbow upward with a clockwise twisting motion. Your opponent's left wrist and elbow should be locked by your hands.

2. Ushiro-katate-dori (rear single-hand seizure)

Method I

Your opponent holds your right arm and is trying to break your right elbow joint with both his hands from the rear. At this time, you should jump a little so that you can release his hold slightly. Simultaneously, hit your opponent's face with your left elbow. Next, turn your body 180 degrees counterclockwise, and pin both of his arms to the left side of your body with your left arm from above. Then, kick his groin with your right knee.

Method II

Your opponent holds your right arm and is trying to break your right elbow joint with both his hands from the rear. Simultaneously, bend your upper body forward, and kick your opponent's groin or leg with your left foot (back kick).

Method III

Your opponent holds your right arm and is trying to break your right elbow joint with both his hands from the rear. Simultaneously, bend your upper body forward, and stretch your right fingers down close to your body. Next, turn your body 180 degrees clockwise, and grasp your opponent's right wrist with your right hand.

172

Twist his right wrist clockwise, using a circular motion. Advance your left foot, and push the back of your opponent's elbow with your left hand (four fingers above) so that he falls down with left zenpo-kaiten-ukemi (falling forward with roll-out).

3. Ushiro-ryote-dori (rear double hand seizure)

Method I

Your opponent grasps both your wrists with both his hands from the rear. Bend your upper body forward, and kick his groin or solar plexus with your left foot (back kick).

Method II

Your opponent grasps both your wrists with both his hands from the rear. Immediately, withdraw your left foot diagonally to a position behind your right foot, and turn your body 180 degrees counterclockwise. Next, kick his groin with your right knee (knee kick).

Method III

Your opponent grasps both your wrists (or upper arms) with both his hands from the rear. Simultaneously, straighten the fingers of both hands. Raise the left arm straight upward. Likewise, straighten the right arm forward so that the fingers are pointing forward. Next, turn your body 90 degrees clockwise, and bring your left hand down to near your left hip so that you pass just under his left armpit, now his left arm is in front of your body. Step diagonally to the right side, and press your opponent's left elbow with your right upper arm so that your opponent falls down on his back (using a right zenpo-kaiten-ukemi).

Method IV

Your opponent grasps both your wrists (or upper arms) with both his hands from the rear. Raise both your arms straight upward and inward. Simultaneously, withdraw your left foot diagonally to the left and withdraw your right foot diagonally to the left so that you pass under his left armpit. Next, bring both your hands downward in front of your stomach. Then, grasp the back of his right hand with your left hand and grasp his right hand with your right hand (kote-gaeshi).

Withdraw your left foot and bring his right wrist upward and twist his right wrist outward with your hands so that he falls down with right zenpo-kaiten-ukemi. After he falls down, grasp his right elbow with your right hand. Pull his right hand to the left and push his right elbow down to the left with your right hand. Therefore, he turns over onto his stomach. Continuously press his right wrist with your left hand and right elbow with your right hand.

177

4. Ushiro-eri-dori (rear collar seizure)

You have no idea whether your opponent is grasping you from the rear with either the right or left hand, so you should turn your body 180 degrees counterclockwise.

Method I

Your opponent is grasping the back of your collar with his right (or left) hand from the rear and is trying to pull you down. Simultaneously, move your left foot diagonally to a position behind your right foot. Turn your body 180 degrees counterclockwise, open your left hand, and cover your face (palm outward) in case your opponent tries to hit you. Next, strike your opponent's face with your right fist.

Method II

Your opponent is grasping the back of your collar from the rear with his right hand. Immediately, move your left foot diagonally to a position behind your right foot. Turn your body 180 degrees counterclockwise, open your left hand, and cover your face (palm outward). Strike your opponent's solar plexus with your right fist.

Next, grasp his right wrist with your right hand and press it to the left side of your neck. Next, bring your left arm up from the left to the right with a circular motion and press the back of his right elbow with your left forearm until he falls down on his stomach. After he falls down on his stomach, you also kneel down (on two knees) in an upright position and press the back of his right elbow with your left forearm and push his wrist with your left shoulder.

Method III

Your opponent is grasping the back of your collar from the rear with his left hand. Immediately, move your left foot diagonally to a position behind your right foot. Turn your body 180 degrees counterclockwise, open your left hand, and cover your face (palm outward). Strike your opponent's face with your right fist. Next, grasp his left wrist with both your hands. Press the back of his left elbow with your right armpit so that you can control your opponent's left arm (hiji-gatame).

Method IV

Your opponent is grasping the back of your collar from the rear with his right hand. Immediately, move your left foot diagonally to a position behind your right foot. Turn your body 180 degrees counterclockwise, open your left hand, and cover your face (palm outward). Strike your opponent's face with your right fist.

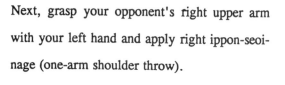
Next, grasp your opponent's right upper arm with your left hand and apply right ippon-seoi-nage (one-arm shoulder throw).

Method V

Your opponent is grasping the back of your collar from the rear with his left hand. Immediately, move your left foot diagonally to a position behind your right foot. Turn your body 180 degrees counterclockwise, open your left hand, and cover your face (palm outward). Strike your opponent's body with your right fist as you grasp your opponent's left wrist or sleeve and apply right ippon-seoi-nage (one-arm shoulder throw).

5. Ushiro-kumi-tsuki (rear body seizure)

Ushiro-kumi-tsuki has two classifications: 1) Ushiro-uchi-kumi-tsuki (rear under arm body seizure), 2) Ushiro-soto-kumi-tsuki (rear over arm body seizure).

1) Ushiro-uchi-kumi-tsuki (rear under arm body seizure)

Method I

Your opponent is grasping your body under the arms from the rear. Immediately, hit your opponent's face with your left (or right) elbow.

Method II

Your opponent is grasping your body under the arms from the rear. Immediately, hit your opponent's face with your right and left elbow. Next, move your right foot to the right so that his right foot is positioned between your legs. Bend your upper body, and grasp your opponent's right ankle with both your hands.

Next, pull his foot toward your chest, and straighten your upper body so that your opponent falls down on his back. Next, kick his groin with your left foot.

If your opponent continues to hold onto you, you may sit on his body and hit his groin with your hand.

Method III

Your opponent is grasping your body under the arms from the rear. Immediately, hit your opponent's face with your left elbow. Next, grasp your opponent's right forearm with both your hands, and hold it tightly in your right armpit. Advance your right foot to a position in front and just a little to the outside of your opponent's right foot.

Throw your body counterclockwise so that your opponent follows you and falls down on his back. You should land on top of your opponent as you both fall down. Then, hit your opponent's solar plexus with your left elbow.

2) Ushiro-soto-kumi-tsuki (rear over arm body seizure)

Method I

    Your opponent is grasping your body over the arms from the rear. You move your hips to the right and quickly hit to the groin with your left knife-hand.

Method II

Your opponent is grasping your body over the arms from the rear. Simultaneously, spread your left arm outside, lower your body, and move your left foot to the left. Immediately, grasp the back of your opponent's left hand with your left hand, and grasp his left wrist with your right hand. Next, move your right foot deeply backward to a position between your left foot and your opponent's left foot. Pass your body under your opponent's left armpit. Then, twist his arm clockwise with both your hands (ude-hineri). At this time, push your opponent's left elbow upward above shoulder level so that he feels pain and cannot move.

Method III

Your opponent is grasping your body over the arms from the rear. Simultaneously, arms bent, elbows to the outside, move them both away from the body. Next, drop your entire body to the ground (at this time, your hips should be near your heels) so that you can escape from his hold. Next, kick your opponent's face with your right foot.

Method IV

Your opponent is grasping your body over the arms from the rear. Simultaneously, arms bent, elbows to the outside, move them both away from the body. Simultaneously, drop your right knee. Next, grasp his right wrist or sleeve with your left hand. Hold his right upper arm tightly with your right upper arm and forearm. Then, pull his right wrist or sleeve forward with your left hand and right arm, and bend your upper body so that he falls down over your right shoulder. After he falls down, you strike his face with your right fist.

Method V

Your opponent is grasping your body over the arms from the rear. Simultaneously, arms bent, elbows to the outside, move them both away from the body. Simultaneously, bend your knees. (At this time, your hips should be near his knees.) Next, grasp his right wrist with your right hand (palm inward), and grasp his left wrist with your left hand (palm inward).

Then, pull his wrists forward with both your hands and bend your upper body so that he falls down over your head. After he falls down, kick his face with your right foot.

6. Ushiro-ryoude-kime (rear double-arm lock)

Method I

Your opponent is trying to lock your arms from the rear. Before he can engage his hands, drop your entire body to the ground so that you can escape from his hold. Next, kick your opponent's face with your right foot.

Method II

Your opponent is trying to lock your arms from the rear. Before he can engage his hands, tighten both your armpits. Next, advance your right foot to a position in front and just a little to the outside of your opponent's right foot.

Throw your body counterclockwise so that your opponent falls down on his back and you are on top of his body. Then, hit your opponent's body with your left elbow.

Method III

Your opponent locks your arms from the rear. Move your hips to the right and withdraw your left foot to behind your right foot. Then, slide your left foot to a position behind his feet so that your left abdomen is behind his right hip. Next, press your opponent's chest with your left arm, and throw your entire body backward so that your opponent falls down on his back.

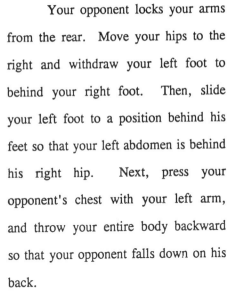

D. Tohma-no-waza (far-front techniques)

When you practice tohma-no-waza, it is important for you to maintain eye contact and the proper distance between you and your opponent. Body movement is also an important part of this practice. Do not oppose your opponent's power directly. Instead, avoid it, and then apply the techniques.

When you are the defender, you are practicing defensive and counterattack movements while your opponent practices his thrusting and kicking techniques. In this way, both of you develop your skill in these movements.

At the beginning of the practice of tohma-no-waza, you and your opponent face each other in the natural stance. Then, you and your opponent simultaneously assume the left fighting stance (hidari shobu-dachi); you effect this by advancing the left foot one pace forward and bending both knees slightly. The toes of your left foot point straight towards your opponent.

The other foot is turned facing 45 degrees to the right. At this time, your body weight is distributed equally on both feet. Your left fist is in front of your eyes just below the eyes (bend your left arm downward slightly), and right fist is in front of your solar plexus. The upper body should be turned slightly to the right. Your entire body should be relaxed. This stance assumed on the opposite side is called right fighting stance (migi shobu-dachi).

The proper distance to stand apart is the distance that it takes for your opponent to move his right foot one step forward and be able to strike with his right hand to your solar plexus or face.

Tohma-no-waza (far-front techniques) are classified as: 1. Chudan-tsuki (middle thrust), 2. Jodan-tsuki (upper thrust), 3. Mae-geri (front kick), 4. Yoko-geri (side kick), 5. Mawashi-geri (round kick), and 6. Ushiro-geri (back kick).

1. Chudan-tsuki (middle thrust)

Method I

You and your opponent assume a left fighting stance (hidari shobu-dachi). Your opponent steps forward with his right foot into right forward stance, while trying to thrust you in the solar plexus with his right fist (chudan-tsuki). Simultaneously, move your right foot backward to avoid your opponent's fist, and block his right forearm from the right to the left with your left forearm. Next, kick your opponent's groin or stomach with your right foot (mae-geri).

Method II

You and your opponent assume a left fighting stance. Your opponent steps forward with his right foot into right forward stance, while trying to thrust you in the solar plexus with his right fist (chudan-tsuki). Simultaneously, move your right foot backward, block your opponent's right forearm from the right to the left with your left forearm, and strike the left side of your opponent's face with your right knife-hand (palm up).

Method III

You and your opponent assume a left fighting stance. Your opponent steps forward with his right foot into right forward stance, while trying to thrust you in the solar plexus with his right fist (chudan-tsuki). Advance your left foot diagonally to the left, and turn your body clockwise so that you avoid his fist. Next, grasp your opponent's right wrist from the outside with your right hand. Hit the front of your opponent's neck with your left knife-hand (palm down). Next, push your opponent backward with your left knife-hand so that your opponent falls down on his back.

Method IV

You and your opponent assume a left fighting stance. Your opponent steps forward with his right foot into right forward stance, while trying to thrust you in the solar plexus with his right fist (chudan-tsuki). Simultaneously, advance your left foot diagonally to the left, turn your body clockwise, and block his right forearm from the left to the right with your left forearm so that you can avoid his fist. Next, hit your opponent's face with your right fist. Then, move your left and right foot to a position behind your opponent, and apply hadaka-jime (naked choke).

Method V

You and your opponent assume a left fighting stance. Your opponent steps forward with his right foot into right forward stance, while trying to thrust you in the solar plexus with his right fist (chudan-tsuki). Simultaneously, move your left foot backward, and block your opponent's right forearm with your left forearm, moving it from the right to the left. Next, bring your left hand behind your opponent's right elbow. At the same time, advance your left foot diagonally to the left, and press his elbow so that your opponent bends his upper body.

Next, hit the back of your opponent's neck with your right knife-hand, and kick your opponent's body with your right knee so that your opponent falls down on his back.

Method VI

You and your opponent assume a left fighting stance. Your opponent steps forward with his right foot into right forward stance, while trying to thrust you in the solar plexus with his right fist (chudan-tsuki). Simultaneously, move your left foot backward, and turn your body to the left. Next, grasp your opponent's right wrist from the inside with both your hands (left hand from above, right hand from underneath). Twist your opponent's arm counterclockwise with both your hands in front of the right side of your face. Advance your left foot diagonally, further than your right foot. Next, turn your body 180 degrees clockwise, and pull your opponent's arm down with both your hands so that your opponent falls down on his back.

Method VII

You assume a left fighting stance. Your opponent assumes a right fighting stance. Then, your opponent steps forward with his left foot into left forward stance, while trying to thrust you in the solar plexus with his left fist (chudan-tsuki). Advance your right foot diagonally to the right. Block and grasp his left forearm (near the wrist) with your left hand from the right to the left. Thrust to the left side of his face with your right fist. At this time, your right forearm is in front of his throat. Advance your right foot behind his feet. Grasp the right side of his shoulder and push backward with your forearm.

Simultaneously, you fall backward so that he falls down on his back. Then, kick his body with your right heel.

2. Jodan-tsuki (upper thrust)

Method I

You and your opponent assume a left fighting stance. Your opponent steps forward with his right foot into right forward stance, while trying to thrust you in the face with his right fist (jodan-tsuki). Simultaneously, move backward with your right foot to avoid your opponent's fist. Immediately, block his forearm with your left forearm from underneath (jodan-uke). Next, kick your opponent's groin or solar plexus with your right foot (mae-geri).

Method II

You and your opponent assume a left fighting stance. Your opponent steps forward with his right foot into right forward stance, while trying to thrust you in the face with his right fist (jodan-tsuki). Simultaneously, advance your right foot diagonally to the right, and immediately block your opponent's right forearm with your left forearm from the right to the left (kake-uke). Next, you thrust the right fist to the face. Advance your right foot between your opponent's feet and turn your body to the left. Next, drop your left knee onto the mat.

Grasp the back of his heel with your left hand from the outside and pull toward you. Simultaneously, strike the inside of your opponent's right knee with your right knife-hand. With the same hand push it so that he falls down on his back. After he falls down, grasp his right ankle with both your hands. You stand up, then, kick his groin with your right foot.

Method III

You and your opponent assume a left fighting stance. Your opponent steps forward with his right foot into right forward stance, while trying to thrust you in the face with his right fist (jodan-tsuki). Simultaneously, move your right foot and upper body to the right side (so that you can avoid his fist). Grasp your opponent's right wrist with your left hand (the four fingers above) from the right to the left. Next, thrust your opponent's throat with your right crescent-hand (mikazukite), and grasp his neck with the same hand. Advance your left foot,

and apply right o-soto-gari (big outside reaping). After he falls down, strike his face with your right fist.

Method IV

You and your opponent assume a left fighting stance. Your opponent steps forward with his right foot into right forward stance, while trying to thrust you in the face with his right fist (jodan-tsuki). Withdraw your right foot to a position behind your left foot, and turn your body 90 degrees clockwise; at the same time, push his right forearm away with your left forearm from the left to the right. Then, step forward deeply with your left foot, and place it behind your opponent's back and right foot. Strike his abdomen with your left elbow.

Next, push your opponent's abdomen with your left upper arm so that your opponent falls down on his back.

Method V

You assume a left fighting stance. Your opponent assumes a right fighting stance, then, steps forward with his left foot into left forward stance, while trying to thrust you in the face with his left fist (jodan-tsuki). Advance your right foot diagonally to the right. Block his left forearm with your left forearm from the right to the left. Then, grasp his left wrist with your left hand. Strike his left elbow with your right forearm. Advance your right foot behind his left foot. Strike the left side of his face diagonally downward with your right elbow. Grasp the right side of his shoulder and push backward with your right arm (your right forearm is in front of his throat) so that you can take his hip joint with your right hand and lower body.

Next, strike his groin or body with your left knife-hand. Your opponent falls down on his back.

Method VI

You and your opponent assume a left fighting stance. Your opponent steps forward with his right foot into right forward stance, while trying to thrust you in the face with his right fist (jodan-tsuki). Immediately, advance your left foot diagonally to the left, and turn your body to the right. Grasp your opponent's right forearm with your left hand from the left to the right. Next, bend your upper body sideways, and put your right hand on the floor to your right.

Immediately, jump in, feet first, and scissor your opponent's body with your legs (put the back of your left leg on your opponent's solar plexus, and put the front of your right leg behind his right and left knees). Next, hit his lower body with the back of your left leg, twist your hips to the left, press your left leg backward, and pull your opponent's right arm downward with your left hand so that your opponent falls down on his back.

Method VII

You and your opponent assume a left fighting stance. Your opponent steps forward with his right foot into right forward stance, while trying to thrust you in the face with his right fist (jodan-tsuki). Immediately, step backward with your left foot, and turn your body 90 degrees counterclockwise. At the same time, grasp your opponent's right forearm with your left hand (the four fingers from above) from the right to the left, and pull your opponent in the direction of his motion. Then, bend both your knees, and advance your right foot between your opponent's feet. Next, insert your right hand between his thighs, and grasp his right thigh from the inside. Your right shoulder should be placed on his right inner thigh. At this time, the back of your head touches your opponent's uniform below the level of the belt.

Next, straighten your knees, and stand up. At this moment, pull your opponent's right arm downward with your left hand, and bring your right shoulder up so that your opponent falls down in front of your left side.

3. Mae-geri (front kick)

Method I

You and your opponent assume a left fighting stance. Your opponent tries to kick you in the groin with his right foot (mae-geri). Step backward with your right foot. At the same time, block your opponent's right foot with your left forearm from the right to the left (gedan-uke). Next, kick his groin with your right foot (mae-geri).

Method II

You and your opponent assume a left fighting stance. Your opponent tries to kick you in the groin with his right foot (mae-geri). Step sideways to the right with your right foot. At the same time, block your opponent's right foot with your left forearm from the right to the left (gedan-uke). Strike his face with your right fist.

Method III

You and your opponent assume a left fighting stance. Your opponent tries to kick you in the groin or solar plexus with his right foot. Step backward with your right foot, and turn your body 90 degrees clockwise. Next, grasp your opponent's right ankle with your left hand in a swinging motion from below, and grasp his right ankle from above with your right hand.

Then, lift your opponent's right leg upward, and push him backward to the mat with both your hands.

Method IV

You and your opponent assume a left fighting stance. Your opponent tries to kick you in the groin or solar plexus with his right foot. Advance your right foot diagonally to the right, turn your body 90 degrees counter-clockwise, and block his kicking foot with your left forearm from the right to the left (gedan-uke). Next, hit the left side of his face with your right knife-hand (palm up).

224

Grasp his right wrist with the left hand. Advance your right foot to a position in front of your opponent's right foot. Pivot so that your toes are pointing in the same direction as your opponent's toes. Next, bend your right knee, lower your body, and encircle your opponent's neck tightly with your right arm. Next, turn your body to the left, moving your left foot in front of your opponent's left foot. Your toes are now pointing in the same direction as your opponent's toes. Your feet are shoulder-width apart, and the knees are bent. Your back is in close contact with the front of your opponent's body. Thrust your hips deeply to the right, past your opponent's right hip. Them, straighten your knees, and twist your upper body forward and to the left, pulling forcefully with your left hand and right arm. Therefore, he falls down on his back. (koshi-guruma.) Strike your opponent's face with your right fist.

Method V

You and your opponent assume a left fighting stance. Your opponent tries to kick you in the groin or solar plexus with his right foot. Advance your left foot diagonally to the left, turn your body clockwise, and block his right kicking foot with your right forearm (gedan-uke) from the left to the right. Next, strike the right side of his face with your left fist.

Then, push your opponent backward with your left forearm. Simultaneously, sweep your opponent's back ankle with your left foot so that your opponent falls down on his back. Next, strike your opponent's face with your right fist.

4. Yoko-geri (side kick)

Method I

You and your opponent assume a left fighting stance. Your opponent tries to kick you in the abdomen with his right side kick (yoko-geri). Advance your left foot diagonally to the left side, and block your opponent's side kick with your right forearm (gedan-uke) in a sweeping motion from the left to the right. Next, hit your opponent's head with your left fist. Then, move your feet behind your opponent, and apply hadaka-jime (naked choke).

228

Method II

You and your opponent assume a left fighting stance. Your opponent tries to kick you in the solar plexus with his right side kick (yoko-geri). Step backward with your right foot, and turn your body 90 degrees clockwise. Grasp your opponent's right ankle with both your hands (right hand from above, left hand from underneath). Next, kick his left knee or groin with your left foot (yoko-geri).

Method III

You and your opponent assume a left fighting stance. Your opponent tries to kick you in the solar plexus with his right side kick. Move your right foot to the right, and block his right leg with your left forearm from the right to the left. Next, you thrust his throat with your right crescent-hand (mikazakite). Advance your right foot between his feet, and push him backward with your right crescent-hand so that he falls down on his back.

Method IV

You and your opponent assume a left fighting stance. Your opponent tries to kick you in the kidney with his right side kick (yoko-geri). Advance your left foot diagonally to the left, and turn your body clockwise. At the same time, block his right leg with your left forearm (chudan-soto-uke) from the left to the right. Advance your right foot to a position behind his left heel and bring your left foot behind your own right foot. Next, grasp his chin with your right hand, and grasp his left shoulder with your left hand (the four fingers on top). Then, pull him backward so that he falls down on his back.

Method V

You and your opponent assume a left fighting stance. Your opponent tries to kick you in the face with his right side kick (yoko-geri). Advance your left foot diagonally to the left and block his right leg with your left forearm from the left to the right. Next, strike his neck with your left knife-hand. Advance your left foot to a position behind his left foot. At this time, the left side of your body should contact the front of his body and the front of your upper leg should contact the back of his upper leg. Grasp his neck and push backward with your left arm so that his hip joint is taken.

Next, strike his solar plexus with your right knife-hand. After the strike, he falls down on his back. Kick his groin with your right foot.

5. Mawashi-geri (round kick)

Method I

You and your opponent assume a left fighting stance. Your opponent kicks toward your face with a right round kick (mawashi-geri). Slide your right foot to the right; also move your body to the right, bend your knees slightly, and block his right round kick with your left forearm (raise your left arm over the left side to cover your face with an upper block). Next, kick his groin with your left foot (mae-geri).

Method II

You and your opponent assume a left fighting stance. Your opponent kicks toward your face with a right round kick (mawashi-geri). Slide your right foot to the right; also move your body to the right, bend your knees slightly, and block his right round kick with your left forearm (raise your left arm over the left side to cover your face with an upper block). Strike his chin with right palm-heel (shotei). Advance your right foot between your opponent's feet. Then, push his chin with your right palm-heel so that your opponent falls down on his back.

Method III

You and your opponent assume a left fighting stance. Your opponent kicks toward your face with a right round kick (mawashi-geri). Withdraw your left foot diagonally to the right, and turn your body to the left. Block his right round kick with your right forearm from the right to the left (jodan-soto-uke, the same as chudan-soto-uke except your forearm is in front of your face). Next, strike his face with your right fist and thrust at his stomach with your left fist.

Method IV

You assume a left fighting stance, and your opponent assumes a right fighting stance. Your opponent kicks toward your face with a left round kick (mawashi-geri). Immediately, move your left foot and upper body to the left, and block his left round kick with your right forearm (raise your right arm over the right side to cover your face with an upper block). Hit the left side of his face with your right forearm, grasp his right arm with your left hand, and apply right hip wheel (koshi-guruma).

Method V

You and your opponent assume a left fighting stance. Your opponent kicks to the left side of your body with a right round kick (mawashi-geri). Move your right foot to the right, and turn your body 90 degrees counterclockwise so that you can avoid his kick. Grasp his kicking leg with both your hands and pull his right leg toward the left side of your chest with both your hands. Next, apply right big inside reaping (o-uchi-gari).

6. Ushiro-geri (back kick)

Method I

You and your opponent assume a left fighting stance. Your opponent turns his body 180 degrees clockwise and prepares to apply a back kick. At this time, advance your left foot slightly and kick the back of his hip with your right foot (mae-geri) so that he falls down on his stomach. Next, kick his body with your left foot.

Method II

You and your opponent assume a left fighting stance. Your opponent kicks toward your solar plexus with a right back kick (ushiro-geri). Advance your left foot diagonally to the left, and block his right back kick with your left forearm from the left to the right (chudan-soto-uke). Next, strike the back of his head with your right fist.

Method III

You and your opponent assume a left fighting stance. Your opponent kicks toward your face with a right back kick (ushiro-geri). Advance your left foot diagonally to the left, and block his right back kick with your left forearm from the left to the right (chudan-soto-uke). Next, strike his neck with your left knife-hand and grasp and pull his neck with your left hand. At the same time, sweep his left leg with your left foot so that he falls down on his back. After he falls down, strike his body with your right fist.

Method IV

You and your opponent assume a left fighting stance. Your opponent kicks toward your face with a right back kick (ushiro-geri). Advance your left foot diagonally to the left, and block his right back kick with your right forearm from the left to the right (kake-uke). Next, strike his head with your left fist. At this time, you are at the back of his body.

242

Next, grasp his face and pull toward you with both your hands so that he falls down on his back. Then, thrust at his face with your right fist.

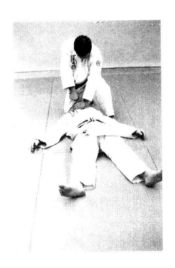

Method V

You and your opponent assume a left fighting stance. Your opponent kicks toward your face with a right back kick (ushiro-geri). Advance your left foot diagonally to the left, and block his right back kick with your left forearm from the left to the right (chudan-soto-uke). Next, kick the back of his left knee with your right foot so that his left knee is on the mat. Bring your right forearm in front of his neck, and choke his neck with both your hands (hadaka-jime).

244

Method VI

You and your opponent assume a left fighting stance. Your opponent kicks toward your face with a right back kick (ushiro-geri). Advance your left foot diagonally to the left, and block his right back kick with your right forearm from the left to the right (kake-uke). Next, strike the back of his neck with your left knife-hand.

Next, bend your body and grasp his left lower leg and pull it with your right hand so that he falls down on his stomach. Then, kick his body with your right foot.

Method VII

You and your opponent assume a left fighting stance. Your opponent kicks toward your face with a right back kick (ushiro-geri). Advance your left foot diagonally to the left, and block his right back kick with your right forearm from the left to the right (kake-uke). At this time, your body is in back of his body.

Then, grasp his groin from the rear with your right hand. Next, pull his groin toward you with your right hand. Simultaneously, push the back of his shoulder with your left hand so that he falls down on his stomach.

Old jujutsu book (densho), author unknown, circa 1750

I wish to thank the following advanced black belt students for assistance in helping me to finish this book: Demonstration partners Kyoshi William Palmer, Kyoshi Satomi Higashi, Shidoin Robin M. Rosenthal (Photographer), Chu-senpai Wesley E. Freeburg, and the students who contributed to this book.